Truth, Lies
&
Propaganda
in Africa
by

Lucinda E Clarke

Truth, Lies and Propaganda

Edited by: Poppy Reid of Purple Sage Editing
Purplesage.editing@gmail.com

Book cover by Rod Craig

This book describes the first part of my journey from primary school teacher, to announcing on the radio, to scriptwriting for radio and television, then into the world of video production.

All the stories are true, although a few names have been changed to protect a couple of the more interesting characters.

If you have ever wondered what goes on behind the camera, this book will let you in on a few secrets and explain how programmes are put together.

What is it like to work with famous people, or interview them when they are not keen to talk to you? Don't be fooled into thinking that working in television is glamorous, it's not. I spent more time in toilets and shuffling through rubbish dumps than I did in banqueting halls.

Making any kind of programme is team work, and I have worked with the best crews and the best studio personnel in South Africa. Without them and their passion, I could not look back with pride on all that we produced.

This book is for them and the clients who placed their faith in us to tell their stories. It is also for my long-suffering husband whose patience while I'm writing has again been stretched to the limit.

No two days are ever the same in the media world and I feel very privileged to have been part of it. Just don't believe everything you see on TV, it's probably wiser not to believe anything at all!

Spain 2014

Contents

1 YOU CAN'T BE A WRITER!

I have decided that tomorrow I am going to kill Caroline. I'd like to squash her flat under a road roller, or push her off the top of the Empire State Building, but I'm not sure how I could get her there, and I suspect Health and Safety have got it securely enclosed by now. I can't shoot her as I've no idea where I'd get a gun, and a knife means getting up close and personal and I don't want her blood all over me. I could poison her, but then I don't know very much about poisons, and I really should dispose of her in a more interesting way. I've grown to hate her, and I want her death to be lingering and painful.

For months she has caused me unmentionable pain and heartache. I've sat up all night worrying about her, and if I give up and go to bed, her very presence has caused me to toss and turn until the early hours. I have to put an end to this. She's got to go. So, how am I going to dispose of her?

A combine harvester, that's the answer!

I will mash her to pieces in a peaceful and idyllic corn field, while the birds sing and the soft wings of the butterflies barely disturb the air. Her screams will resonate as she is dismembered into bite-sized chunks between the rotating blades and her blood spurts metres into the air turning the ripened, golden maize a brilliant red.

Yes, that's what I'll do tomorrow.

For as long as I can remember I have wanted to be a

writer. In those early days, it seemed such a glamorous occupation, I so admired those people who could transport others into a land of fantasy, take them back in time to another world or forward into the future on another planet. What was more, you, the writer, were in control! You could give your characters a headache, or better still, break their legs or pop them into a wheelchair, and you could kill them off in so many different and exciting ways.

How about leaving them to be gnawed to death by rats, or drowning them in a vat of vintage wine, or poisoning them with their own birthday cake?

Of course you can be nice to your characters as well. You can present *her* with a loving, rich, faithful and successful husband and four adorable children just like those in 'Little House on the Prairie', and make her stunningly beautiful at the same time. Now she's beginning to sound nauseating, and you hate her already don't you?

It's time to make things go wrong. Enter the nymphomaniac, blonde secretary with the very, very, short skirt barely covering her knickers, legs that start at her armpits, big boobs and a predatory nature. Now, that's more exciting isn't it?

As a child, I had very little control over my life so writing was extra important to me. It was the only way I could escape from the misery of everyday life. I would sit in my room and scribble silly little stories in an exercise book and then run and show them to my mother. She was not kind, and sneered at my earliest attempts to influence the world of books - although my grandfather, a reluctant writer himself, was more encouraging.

A huge influence on me in those days was Jo in 'Little Women'. I can't remember how many times I read Louisa May Alcott's story. Jo began writing when she was young, and I cheered for her when she sold a story and bought a carpet for the house, and then another story which helped keep the family comfortable in difficult times while their father was away fighting in some war or other. (At least that is what we were told. He wouldn't have run off with another woman would he? Or been serving time?) Jo was the heroine of the family for me, and I dreamed of making a fortune by writing such wonderful books that everyone wanted to read them.

Of course life isn't like that, and the usual questions came up as I reached the last of my school years.

"Do you want to be a secretary, a nurse, or a teacher?"

Frankly I didn't want to be any of them. My vision of secretarial work was being a lackey to some overbearing, loud-mouthed man in some dingy office. I would be sent to collect his dry cleaning, sharpen his pencils and spend hours thumping away at a typewriter making thousands of mistakes. I would never make a good secretary. Even today, I'm ashamed to say, I can't touch type, my eyes are constantly glued to the keys, and even at my advanced age I still make thousands of mistakes.

Nursing was a definite no-no. I fainted at the sight of blood, not a prerequisite for a medical career, you'd agree. Even in primary school they sent for my mother to come and take me home after I had fainted in class. The doctor was called, and I was put to bed for the rest of the day. And what had been the cause of all this? It was the human nervous system. The teacher had told us to open our biology books at page such and such and there, in bright, luridly coloured pictures, we could see what happens when you prick your finger. They showed the path taken by messages as they sped to the brain along the nerve highways and back again, armed with the new information that 'Ow! That hurt!'

I even feel a bit queasy now just writing about it.

I collapsed several more times in high school, each time

they decided to rip open a heart, an eyeball or some hapless animal's lung. But the results were less dramatic and I was no longer in the spotlight for my disgraceful behaviour. The teacher simply instructed two of the biggest lads to grab me under the armpits, drag me through the door, and prop me up against the outside wall of the biology lab.

So that left teaching. I agreed to become a teacher as it seemed the least daunting career that could possibly be suitable. Not that I had any experience of children, they were about as foreign to me as the pygmies in the Congo. However, I convinced myself that teachers had nice long holidays, and they finished work early at three o'clock every afternoon.

I tried one more time, but my last few whines about wanting to be a writer were firmly ignored, and that was that. Dickens, the Brontë sisters and Shakespeare would never have to turn in their graves worrying that I would pose any threat to their sales revenues.

As the obedient daughter, I would attempt to pour information into the heads of unwilling and recalcitrant children and earn a proper and respectable living.

I did venture out in my late teens and wrote a small piece for our church newsletter, which they printed, but they were probably very desperate to fill the pages. I have no recollection what I wrote about now, but most likely it was a report on the Sunday school where I was teaching at the time.

I was being totally hypocritical as I'd almost stopped believing in God and I was just gathering brownie points in my attempt to get into teacher training college. It was also a good chance to meet some children and get acquainted with a few of these little aliens.

At the time I was so thrilled, and I sneaked an extra few copies of the magazine from the back of the church and read my article over and over again. I vowed to keep it for posterity, and practised signing my name at the bottom, ready to hand out to the long, admiring queue of fans, impatient to receive their own personal signed copy of my masterpiece.

Strange, I've no idea what happened to all those copies I carefully hid under the bed.

So I remained undiscovered for years, and I still am if I'm completely honest, but look who's in charge here. I'm the writer, remember? But I guess I'd better stick to the truth with only a limited amount of literary licence.

I did have one success in school, when we were asked in the English class to put together a report as an eye witness to some disaster. I must have been in the second year in high school and I chose to record the destruction of one of the rockets taking people into space. It was all the rage in those days, going into space that is. In my mind I watched it go racing into the sky, only to freeze for a second, and then come crashing back down to earth again.

I poured my heart and soul into my essay, pretending I had been sent to Houston by The London Times to report on this momentous event, although obviously they were not expecting the crash. For my purpose that was a bonus.

I was so impressed with my efforts I bounced around in class waiting to be awarded an A+. I had even set up a mirror in my bedroom and practiced my responses in accepting the teacher's praises with genuine humility and a *savoir faire* shrug of the shoulders.

Her praises never came. Instead, she accused me of plagiarism.

"What newspaper did you copy this from?" she demanded, hovering over me like a hungry raptor. Well, it was not exactly my fault that just the previous week a rocket really *had* crashed to earth, but I was only vaguely aware of that fact. You don't watch the news much when you're a teenager.

I glanced round the classroom, seeing rows of grinning ex-friends who were thoroughly enjoying my discomfort. The more I denied it, the more the English teacher disbelieved me. I was not only a plagiarist but now I was a liar as well. She tore my report into a hundred pieces, (I'm throwing in a bit of literary licence here), which fluttered down onto my desk like confetti.

Well that was quite enough to curtail my enthusiasm; not for writing, but for any attempt to produce anything special for her ever again. Like many other students in the class, I scribbled mediocre rubbish for each assignment and accepted a range of B grades as my lot.

It never occurred to me that if she thought I'd lifted it from the local newspaper, I had written a good report. I wish I'd realized it at the time, but my spirit was crushed. What made me really cross was that years later, I heard she'd told my mother she always knew I had talent in English and would succeed as a writer. Nonsense! She never thought any such thing.

And so the years went on. I qualified as a teacher, taught children, some adorable, some monsters, and some whose hygiene was questionable. I worked hard and there are probably a few hundred people rattling around in the world today that can read and write thanks to my valiant efforts. There were even many days when I enjoyed my work, and I really did my best.

Fleetingly, I would think of my past ambition to set the world of books on fire, but I was usually too tired at the end of the day to put pen to paper. What happened to this knocking off at three o'clock rubbish? And those month long holidays that flew past?

Occasionally, I would try and put a story together, but I found my thoughts ran so much faster than my pen, and the manuscript contained so many crossings out, and arrows redirecting words into their proper places, and paragraphs I wanted rearranged, it was impossible to read anything. I changed from pen to pencil, and used an eraser, but that didn't help either. I was left with a dull grey soggy mess and holes in the paper where I'd pressed too hard.

I even gave up practising my speech for when I won the Nobel Prize for Literature. I would give up my dreams of writing and accept what was practical and sensible.

2 RADIO LIBYA

I buried my literary dreams and forgot about them, and it wasn't until a few years later when I was living in Benghazi in Libya, and teaching at the local school, a friend suggested I try out for the local radio station.

"Go on radio? You've got to be kidding!"

"No, really, I mean it," said Anne. "I heard about it on the English Language Service. They're looking for new presenters and I applied and they've taken me on."

From four until seven every weekday, we were privileged to have three hours of radio on the national network in English. Harmless stuff to be sure, a news broadcast carefully controlled by the authorities in Tripoli, the Libyan capital, and re-runs bought cheaply from the BBC of riveting series such as the 'Paul Temple Mysteries', 'Men from the Ministry', and 'The Navy Lark'.

I think the Libyans believed these programmes were a true reflection of British politics and the armed forces. The humour totally escaped them and I suspect they saw these as quite serious programmes, only acknowledging the stupidity of life in Britain. There was no canned laughter to give them a clue either. I suspect they chuckled to themselves at getting us to cheerfully introduce programmes which showed us up in a ridiculous light.

Feeling more than a little self conscious, I drove myself to the entrance of the radio station the following afternoon. Next to the barrier defending the car park was a soldier, complete with a large gun, who peered at me through the window of my scruffy VW Beetle. I explained in my atrocious Arabic that I had an appointment to see the station chief for an audition.

He either didn't understand me, or he didn't believe me, and left me sitting there sweltering in the heat, while he disappeared into his little hut and picked up the phone. Eventually he came out, reluctantly raised the barrier, and pointed to a space where I should park my car. As I manoeuvred my dented vehicle into the narrow gap, I noticed that mine was the only down market model in sight. My old Beetle cowered among the BMWs and Mercedes, but I was cheered to see that most of them also had dents and scrapes in the bodywork. Driving was not the safest occupation in Libya. In fact, if you had a dent-free car, you were considered something of a sissy or a wuss.

I looked around, with no idea where to go. I was surrounded on either side by low, single storey buildings which didn't even have signs in Arabic, much less English. I looked back at the guard on the gate, but he was no longer in sight, and then came the call to prayers. This was a bit tricky as with the delay at the gate I was already late for my appointment, and now I would have to hover around waiting until after everyone had finished facing east and had rolled up their prayer mats.

Eventually I made my way into the building on the left and, if I'd thought it looked scruffy on the outside, the inside was even worse. A long corridor stretched from one end to the other, with cream and green walls separated by a thick brown line half way up. The paint was peeling off the doorframes on either side of the corridor and the rough stone floor looked as if it had never met a mop or a broom.

I crept down the passage, looking right and left, hoping that I would meet someone to show me the way. I was beginning

9

to have grave misgivings about the whole idea and I was just about to turn round and leave, when a voice barked out to me through an open doorway.

"Audition?" he shouted.

"Uh, yes."

The man behind the desk rose and marched out, fluttering his hands in the air to indicate I should follow him. Three doors further along he grabbed the handle and flung it open to reveal a small room. The walls were covered with white bison board full of holes, and there was a table, a chair and a microphone hanging from the ceiling. He pointed imperiously to the chair and tentatively I walked in and sat down.

Looking around, I saw that part of the wall in front of me was made of glass, and on the other side sat an engineer behind another suspended microphone. He gave me the thumbs up, and I nodded and waited.

Time passed and nothing happened, until my guide waved his arms which I took to be an invitation to start speaking. But what was I going to say? Every thought flew straight out of my head, my tongue felt five times its normal size and my mouth went dry.

"Audition, audition," I mumbled to myself. "Say something you idiot. My name is Lucinda," I croaked, "and I have come here today for an audition. I uh, um, live here in Benghazi and I uh, um, teach at the local school and um, uh, I...." I then dried up completely. What else could I tell them? That we brewed illegal beer, held parties, constructed secret stills making pure alcohol, or that we camped on the beach and went skinny dipping after dark? No, not a good idea, we might not be on the same wavelength, and that wouldn't go down too well.

The man in the doorway nodded and then gestured for me to follow him. He led me to another office at the far end of the corridor; knocked briefly, opened the door and I followed him inside. This office was quite the smartest I had seen so far, I guessed it must be inhabited by the Big Boss.

Sure enough, there behind the desk sat an even larger man, in a smart blue nightshirt, smoking furiously and swigging from a bottle, containing, I'm sure, nothing more lethal than cold tea, despite the Jonny Walker label on the outside.

The men rattled away in rapid Arabic and then the Big Boss told me to sit down. To my amazement, his English was perfect.

"So why do you want to be an announcer?"

There was only one problem with that question. By now I was quite sure that I *didn't* want to be an announcer. I had little desire to make a total idiot of myself with all my friends listening in to hear me um, and er, and uh, and ah my way through every evening. I played goldfish for several seconds and then gave some fatuous reply, I really can't remember what.

"You have passed the audition," replied the Big Boss, to my total amazement. Surely he was joking! It was perfectly obvious their standards were just below zero, or they were absolutely desperate. "But you will have to write your own links," he added.

The word 'write' permeated my stunned brain. Did he say write? And they were going to pay me? To write? Then this was my chance! I perked up. Now I *did* want the job. I gave him what I thought was my best smile, but in return he looked rather startled, so perhaps it was more of a leer, and that would never do in an Arabic country. I might get flung out before my radio career had begun. I tried the humble approach.

"I would be very, very grateful for the opportunity," I mumbled, then remembered that radio announcers were supposed to sound sharp and crystal clear. "Thank you so much," I shouted. "When do I start?"

He backed away in his chair and gave me another startled look.

"The day after tomorrow, be here at half past three," and with that, he dismissed me.

As I walked back along the corridor and out into the blinding heat, I reasoned that forty eight hours was not a long time to prepare for my radio debut. And what did he want me to write? I thought I'd better have a chat with Ann and find out.

"What do I write?" I asked Anne when I popped into her house on the way home.

"The links," she replied.

"Links? You're not talking about golf courses are you?"

"No, stupid. The links are the bits between the programmes."

"Oh, I sort of introduce them?" I was pleased that I had caught on so quickly. I *am* bright, I told myself. Then I had another thought. "How do I know what programmes they're going to broadcast?"

"The Big Boss didn't tell you anything?"

"Uh, no. I'm not sure we forged a long and meaningful relationship."

"In the production office there are pigeon holes and you will find a box of tapes in the one marked English Broadcast, along with a running order. Look to see what is going to be on and then you quickly scribble down a few words to say what is coming next. It's easy!"

"Hmmm, doesn't sound too difficult."

"Tell you what. Come in with me tomorrow and I'll show you the ropes. Can you get a babysitter?"

The next afternoon, sure enough there were the tapes sent down from Tripoli nestling contentedly in their wooden

12

pigeonhole, and Ann showed me what to do. It did seem simple, any child could do this and even the chance to write a little was magic, people would hear me reading *my words*. I was over the moon.

I was yet to discover how repetitive those words would become night after night after night. There are only so many ways you can introduce another 'Paul Temple Mystery', for example, especially as they were not sent down in the correct order so you had no idea of the content. Episode three might follow episode five, then seven and back to three again followed by programme sixteen. It made little sense to the listeners anyway.

But the radio station was paying us a fortune, and this was money for jam. I looked forward to my first shift the following day and arrived at least half an hour early, to prepare and compose both myself and my script.

It was just as well I did. As I walked into the production office, I could see from the far end that the pigeonhole designated for the English programmes was empty.

I raced down the corridor to Big Boss's office. It was also empty. I then went up and down the corridor, looking for anyone who could help me. As none of the doors were open, I took the liberty of looking inside each one, I was that desperate. Eventually I found myself in the control room.

"No tapes from Tripoli," I hissed at the controller.

He looked up in alarm, thought for a moment and then said, thankfully in English. "Make it up."

"Make it up! Make what up?" I asked.

"Play music," he smiled at me.

"Music?" This was getting more bizarre by the moment.

"Record library there," he pointed down the corridor then looked at his watch. "Be quick, on air soon."

I raced out of the control room and by opening the remaining doors along the corridor, found a room with floor to ceiling shelves on which nestled hundreds and hundreds of records. I began to take them off the shelves at random, reasoning that I should choose a varied mix.

Just as I was about to leave, I saw a large notice pinned on the back of the door.

"THESE ARTISTS DO NOT PLAY!!!!!" it screamed. There was a very, very long list of names. I glanced down at the pile of records I was clutching and saw that just about every one of them was a 'do not play' artist. Frantically I stuffed them back on the shelves and grabbed a few more, racing back to the door each time to ensure the group or singer was not on the forbidden list.

I now had twenty minutes before I was live on air to sort the disks, write the intro and instruct the controller. There simply wasn't enough time. I would have to improvise. As fast as I could, I scribbled down what I hoped was an exciting introduction to say that today we were going to have a thrilling change and listen to some great music of all kinds and so on and so on.

I then put the records in one pile and kept the covers in a separate pile, delivered the disks to the control engineer, and flung myself into the studio next door. As the introductory music blared through my headphones I was still gasping for breath, and I twirled my hand round and round at the guy on the other side of the glass window to indicate that I wanted it repeated. He grinned and nodded.

I panicked again for several seconds, as I couldn't find the 'cut off button' Ann had told me about. You pushed it down to take you off air, for example if you wanted to cough, or shuffle papers. Ah, there it was, under the record covers. I pressed it and cleared my throat, quite forgetting that you had to keep it depressed to cut off the sound. So my first ever radio debut was me coughing my guts up, while the engineer was killing himself laughing in the next room.

I pointed to the record on the top of the pile and waved the cover wildly and helpfully Mamud - I was to learn his name only after the show - put it on the turntable. I then quickly read down the list of tracks and held up five fingers. He was a bright lad and cued up the fifth track. I then proceeded to read the blurb straight off the record sleeve, which was necessary since I'd never heard of the group and I hadn't the faintest idea what their music was like.

Breathlessly I made my introduction, remembering just in time to start with the station call sign, and away we went. The following three hours were nerve-wracking. To my horror I discovered that I had not collected enough records, for up until then I had had no idea that most songs only last about three minutes, a fact that had never permeated my brain. In all, I would need over fifty albums to keep us going until seven o'clock and sign off.

I was so relieved when the time came to introduce the news transmitted direct from Tripoli the capital, as it gave me a break to race back to the library and collect more records. Unfortunately, this time I didn't notice that I'd included a banned artist, and he got played as well, and it was only as I was replacing the disks on the shelves that I noticed what I'd done. I had no idea why some singers were banned while others were acceptable, and it was only much later I discovered that if they'd ever performed, or sold in Israel, they were *persona non grata* in Libya.

That first evening was hell, and I was on the point of giving up altogether, reckoning that this would be among the shortest radio careers in history, until I thought of the glamour, and the money, and the buzz, and the money.

Despite the panic, it *was* a buzz, a total feeling of euphoria, being constantly on the alert, thinking several things at the same time. I was hooked.

If I'd thought things couldn't get worse, I was wrong. There was the evening when having introduced one of the half-hour serials, I had popped back to the production office for a quick cigarette. We always left a radio on in there so we could listen to what was going out on air. It took me several seconds to realize that the radio was silent. I picked it up and turned it on and off - still nothing. I gave it a good shake (things often didn't work in Libya), still nothing. I grabbed new batteries out of the drawer and inserted them. Still nothing.

I flew out of the door and ran down to the control room. There was no sign of Mamud he'd obviously gone out for a smoke as well, but on the console there was the tape still spinning, round and round, and round, going nowhere. It had broken. Noticing some Sellotape on the side I ripped off a piece, spliced the tape together and re-threaded it. Bingo, it worked, and we were back on the air.

On another occasion, we went silent again. It's called 'dead air', and this time Mamud was there in the control room. He was praying, quite oblivious to the fact that the tape had parted company and was spinning like a top. I had a hard time stepping over him to try and repair the damage, terrified that if I nudged him accidently then his deity might be very cross indeed.

I committed the biggest sin of all later that same evening, as I apologised to the listeners for the break in transmission, repeating what I'd heard in my younger days on the BBC, words to the effect that:

"We apologise for the break in transmission earlier this evening, which was due to a technical fault." I was rather pleased with myself, it was the professional thing to do, and I'd taken the initiative.

But the Big Boss didn't think so. I was summoned to his office after the show and given a strong dressing down.

"We never, ever, apologise!" he screamed at me. "You are never, ever to shame the Libyan Arab Jamahiriya

Broadcasting Corporation! Do you understand?"

Frankly I didn't, I couldn't see the shame in basic good manners, but I promised not to commit the sin again.

As the years went on I became more adventurous and much to Ann's horror proposed to the Big Boss that I vary the nightly fare by offering new programmes such as book readings and maybe a quiz as well. Little did I know, I was biting off more than I could chew.

The book reading went quite well to begin with, except the Big Boss chose the book 'The Old Man and the Sea' by Ernest Hemingway. I had never read it before and as it was a classic, I looked forward to serving it up in chunks for nightly broadcast. Oh dear, is there a more depressing book out there? It took weeks and weeks to plough through the whole thing, night after night after night. The feedback I had from listeners was that they were equally bored with it as well, and it made them feel down just hearing about this poor old fisherman who doesn't catch anything at all for days and days and days. Then he hooks a gigantic marlin but as he's taking it back to shore, it's gobbled up by sharks so it's worth nothing by the time he reaches land.

"It's really too miserable to listen to as I prepare supper," many people said.

"Can't you sort of précis it and wrap it up in a couple of sentences?"

"I have to switch the radio off at tea time now, the children keep bursting into tears."

"Would anyone notice if you swapped books and read something different?"

But having started, I could hardly leave the Old Man out there festering in the ocean. I ploughed on manfully and only the Big Boss seemed pleased with my efforts, certainly the audience was less than enthusiastic.

The quiz brought more squawks from the local English-speaking population.

I had discovered a paperback copy of the 'Top of the Form' radio quiz programme in the English bookshop, listing all the questions, with, thank God, the answers in the back. I rounded up participants from the expat community who promised in groups of four to come into the studio and take part in the show.

How difficult could it be? The questions were aimed at fourth and fifth form school kids, say fifteen years old, and it would be a great chance for the contestants to show off their knowledge in public over the airwaves. I mean, who could resist the opportunity to impress all their friends? I had a whole list of eager contestants, not only did they want to win, they also wanted to see inside the studios.

From the outset it was a disaster. In the first week, between them the four participants only answered a total of seven questions correctly. The second week was even worse, a total of five questions. It became more and more embarrassing as I chirped, "At the end of round three, so and so has nil, such and such has nil, it and it also has nil and him and him has one, so him and him is in the lead. Well done him and him!"

Those future contestants who had tuned in to assess their chances of showing off in the later rounds began to rebel. They protested that if I thought they were going to make fools of themselves in front of the whole community, I was very much mistaken.

"But you promised!" I whined. "You said you would come on the show! I can't cancel it after two rounds! Please!"

"You didn't cancel 'The Old Man and the Sea' when we asked you!"

"That was different, the Big Boss chose that and I couldn't get out of it. Please come on the show!"

But all friends have their limits, and in the end the only way round it was to pre-record the show and, I hate to admit it now, cheat. To appease my conscience, I would gently slide the question paper across the table where the answers were boldly underlined in day-glow yellow highlighter. Sadly I had one contestant who didn't get the point of this and at the end of the show, she was the only one who didn't get almost full marks.

As we were recording three shows at a time, I was not prepared for the final show which, much to everyone's horror, was won by a snotty young man who was over in Libya, lecturing at the Garyounis University in some bizarre subject. He and I had nearly come to blows over several answers he gave. He of course knew *all* the answers and sneered at us slightly older folk who struggled to remember what we'd been taught in primary school. And it always seemed to be the case that he got the easy questions as well, the ones we *all* knew. Even I was aware that the lead in pencils is not real lead, so what was it? I asked him.

"C, with a hexagonal dihexagonal dipyramidal crystal symmetry, under the Strunz classification of 01.CB.05a," he answered with a decided snigger.

I mean you can see what we were up against can't you? But I had him this time.

"Wrong!" I chortled. "Anyone else know the answer? Julia?"

"It's not lead, but graphite," she replied with a huge smile.

And then the fight started. It appeared that Big Head had quoted the chemical symbol for graphite, C, which it shares with diamonds and soot, and so to be quite clear, he had included its classification in his answer. This was of course long before the days of the quick check-up on Google, but I tried to stand firm.

"Sorry, I am only allowed to accept the answer I have on the card," I said cheerfully. "Well done Julia."

19

"It's my point, and I want it," sneered Big Head. "And, even if you are supposed to be running the show, you can't change and make up the rules as you go along."

I looked at Julia's crestfallen face. It was the only question she had got right so far, (I'd removed the cheat sheet for the finals), and it seemed cruel to deprive her of her only point. Big Head was several dozen points in the lead even if you added everyone else's score together, but he was not about to let this one slip through his fingers.

I couldn't prove he had the right answer, he might as well have answered the question in Chinese for all the sense it made to me, so I tried the old 'Solomon of the Bible' wisdom and gave them each a point. Big Head sulked for the rest of the programme.

Of course he won the whole series.

We were recording four shows in the final afternoon instead of the usual three, I was so terrified that I would never get the contestants within a mile of the studios again, so I had no physical prize to actually award.

I asked the engineer to stop recording, while I explained the situation.

"I have not yet purchased the prize," I said, "but I will be going to the English Bookshop this afternoon and buying a very nice stainless steel Parker pen. In the meantime we will just have to pretend, and I'll use this ruler as a prop. Everyone OK with that?"

While Big Head might have possessed extensive knowledge when it came to quiz shows, he had zilch imagination when it came to real life.

"You want to present me with a chewed up old ruler?" he sniffed.

"Well it's only a prop for now, it's temporary, I will give you the pen tomorrow, only I haven't got it here right now." I thought even a pre-schooler would understand this.

"And you want me to accept this?" his top lip curled.

"Just pretend for now," I began to whine. "Tomorrow you will get your real prize."

"Haven't you got something nicer to offer me?" He really didn't get it, did he?

"Well I could 'pretend' with this pencil, or a piece of paper, or..." I looked around, there wasn't much extraneous stuff in the studio.

"I'm not impressed at all," Big Head grumbled, glaring at the other smirking contestants.

"Well it's all I have for now," I snapped, "so I am going to present you with this beautiful, stainless steel Parker pen, and you are going to graciously accept, and we are going to record it."

"But you're really going to give me a dog-chewed, wooden ruler," he obviously wanted to make sure he understood the situation completely.

"Bingo. This is radio, so no one will see, and it doesn't really matter what I give you now, you'll get your proper prize tomorrow."

I'm sure the recording no longer exists, but this prize giving ceremony must be the most lack lustre of all time. Big Head sounded positively disgusted with his beautiful, stainless steel pen, and even after a second and third take, he failed to sound more enthusiastic, so I had to leave it at that.

Needless to say, our Top of the Form series was never, ever repeated.

Despite all this, I thoroughly enjoyed my time on the radio. Writing the links was easy, I grew more confident, and the money was good, very good. There was only one more occasion when I wondered if I had made a big mistake.

It was the afternoon of one September 1st, a special day in Libya marking the anniversary of the day Colonel Qadhafi had seized power, and I was lying on the beach when there was a massive explosion from the direction of the harbour. Instantly, there were rumours that Mu'ammar al-Qadhafi himself was in town to inspect the Libyan Navy.

Libyan Navy? As far as any of us knew, the Libyan Navy in Benghazi only had one speed boat about sixteen feet long! No one else was allowed to have a boat any longer than twelve foot. That would be just too humiliating for the navy, wouldn't it?

But it was surprising that Qadhafi was in this part of Libya at all. He was usually thought to be more at ease in Tripoli, or the area known as the Fezzan. Benghazi is in Cyrenaica, which extends eastwards right up to the Egyptian border and it was rumoured to be way out of his comfort zone.

I didn't feel too comfortable either hearing that explosion. Had someone attempted to blow up our beloved leader? We'd all read 'The Hilton Assignment' by Patrick Abram Seale, which documented several attempts on Qadhafi's life, in which the British were intimately involved. The book had been smuggled in at some point, and passed around surreptitiously in a plain, brown, paper cover. It reminded me of the excitement and giggles at school, over a similarly concealed copy of 'Lady Chatterley's Lover', which did the rounds during maths class. There was never any need to read the whole book of course, just simply balance it in the palm of your hand and the pages containing the naughty bits fell open as if by magic. It saved so much time ploughing through the clean, boring bits.

Back to the beach, where I reluctantly rolled up my beach towel and prepared to go to the radio station.

Qadhafi himself had seized power in a bloodless coup by occupying army barracks, police stations and radio stations in Tripoli and Benghazi. He then used the radio to impose his coup, telling everyone to stay indoors and that he was now in charge. Well without going into a history lesson, it was something like that. My point is, I knew that Colonel Qadhafi was a little jittery about radio stations and the power they could impose on the people.

I had every right to be nervous that evening, for as soon as I arrived at the barrier, I was met by a plethora of soldiers who pointed long guns with fixed bayonets at me, and marched either side of my car as I nervously drove into a parking bay. They bounced around on their feet as I slowly got out of the car, followed me in formation into the building and along the corridor to the production office. They jostled so closely that I could smell their breath and the sweat emanating from under their armpits. They did not let up for a second.

As one, we all walked first to the production office where I collected the tapes, and then on to the studio where we all crowded into the small room as I nervously perched on my chair. Through the glass, I noticed that Mamud looked decidedly green. He had his own personal armed guards as well, and was also very nervous. My voice shook as the intro music died away, and it took me three attempts to read the station call sign. Sweat was dripping off my face, despite the air conditioning, and I nearly had a heart attack when I felt one of the bayonets come to rest on my right shoulder. I could feel the end of the steel point gently pricking my skin as I stumbled on, announcing the programmes for the evening, hardly able to read the hastily scrawled script I was writing as I went along. There was so much sweat dripping off me that the cue sheet became quite soggy and the ink started to run.

As soon as the first tape began playing, it was a half-hour comedy from England that was so old I suspected the tape would very soon part company. I was suddenly aware that nature was calling me very loudly indeed. I simply 'had to go.' How did I explain this to a crowd of soldiers who probably didn't speak a word of English? I moved away to my left and slowly stood up. I could think of no sign language that would indicate what I had in mind, well, not without being totally lewd.

I slid towards the door, and like a bunch of monkeys following a banana, they crowded round me as I fled towards the loos. Outside the washroom door, I pointed to the 'ladies' sign and held up my hand to stop them coming any further. I opened the door, raced inside and locked myself in a cubicle, or rather I *would* have done had there been any locks on the doors.

They took no notice of my instructions as they all crowded in behind me and I spent a few very uncomfortable moments, with my foot firmly jammed against the door, until nature and I had finished communicating. I marched out and glared at them as I went to wash my hands, but if they were aware of my feelings they ignored them.

This was disrespect on a grand scale for an Arab male and I began to seethe with anger. How dare they! What were they expecting me to do? If I'd suddenly announced a coup, they wouldn't have a clue, so were they there to intimidate me, just in case? If I'd announced that Colonel Qadhafi was the best thing since sliced bread, they wouldn't have a clue about that either.

It was the longest three hours I have ever experienced, and by the time I got back into my car and drove out of the car park, I was a limp bundle of rags, with only my clothes holding me together.

"You sounded a bit off on the radio tonight," several people commented.

"Not your usual chirpy self then? Bit hung over?"

"Ha ha, sounded as if you were auditioning for Emmanuelle, with all that heavy breathing and gasping," was another comment I did not appreciate.

At least one good thing came out of the attempted coup, if

24

that's what it was, we never did find out. Recently we'd been handed the news to read out live, and while I was slightly aware in those days that each country liked to boast about its own achievements and play down its shortcomings, I was beginning to get decidedly rattled about the stuff they shoved in front of our noses.

"Today the infidels in the British Isles have perfidiously stated that along with their lying, scheming cousins across the Atlantic, they will renege on their empty promises to ......" You get the drift? I had been on the point of refusing to read out any more hate speech on the news, but luckily the harbour incident led to the news items being pre-recorded in Tripoli again and broadcast from there.

It wasn't particularly comfortable being part of an evening's entertainment that broadcast vicious propaganda, but heck the money was so good, and all the presenters explained at great length that we had no control whatsoever over the station policy. And if we all resigned, what would happen then? No English language service at all. Wisely, we all kept our mouths shut.

I had not been in Benghazi all that long when I learned something I had never been aware of before. It was being broadcast overseas that there was a raging war going on between Libya and Egypt. There was blood running down the streets, people being hacked to death on every corner and total mayhem with everyone's lives in danger.

Relatives of several of our friends were making frantic phone calls to work places or sending telegrams, (there were no private phones in our houses), asking if their loved ones were all right.

We all looked up and down the streets, but could see nothing out of the ordinary. Fighting? What fighting? It was all peaceful and quiet. Well hardly quiet there was the usual chaos on the roads, but nothing new.

25

We normally listened to the BBC World Service every evening, but now we began to tune in to Voice of America, Russia Today, Radio Swiss and even Radio Vatican City. And the reports we heard about the situation in our city were as different as it was possible to hear. Who was telling the truth? Where had they got their information from?

I didn't know it then, but this was my first early inkling of the world of propaganda. Hadn't we all been brought up in Britain to believe that everyone in Europe listened in to the BBC World Service during World War II to get the *real* truth? Was it? That's what we had always been told, but was that what they wanted us to believe? I had a lot more to learn, but the world of propaganda was just waiting for me.

Being on air while hugely pregnant was a bit of a problem. I was fine as long as her 'babyship' didn't kick too hard, but a couple of times I was heard to go "uh!" or "ug!" on air. I also had to sit a bit further away from the table as my tummy got larger and larger and I didn't dare touch the microphone which dangled precariously from the ceiling. I had to increase the volume quite a bit and try to avoid shouting at the same time.

I learned years later that I was a bit of a nightmare for the sound engineers, as I have a very quiet voice and they always had to turn their volume control buttons up as high as they would go.

Apart from that one instance, I enjoyed my time working on the radio, though how I fitted it all in with teaching during the mornings, business entertaining in the evenings, bringing up two children, and our frenetic social life, I shall never know. I seemed to have an inexhaustible amount of energy, but again I didn't know what was in store for me years later.

I do remember one evening when we had been entertaining some foreign business guests over from France.

They had brought me two beautiful Dior scarves, and waited until after dinner to hand them over. They were a little puzzled at first as to why I didn't seem too thrilled with their gift as I just sat in the chair and did not respond. It was only as I began to snore loudly did they realize I had fallen asleep at the dinner table.

All good things come to an end and after five and a half years we left Libya, had a brief spell back in the United Kingdom, and we were on our way to Botswana. Then it was back into the classroom and my dreams of becoming a writer, or working again in the media, faded into the background. It had been fun while it lasted, and I persuaded myself that I'd had my brief time in the spotlight, and now it was all over.

Botswana did not have any English language programmes on air, and only if you lived in the south around Gabarone could you tune in to Radio Springbok, broadcast from Johannesburg in South Africa.

After almost three years teaching in Botswana, plus bringing up two young children, running the worst riding school in the world, and keeping track of an errant job-hopping husband, we moved country again. This time it was to South Africa and I was back in another classroom. I had no further thoughts of becoming a writer, and once again my literary ambitions remained a distant memory.

Until the day I was fired.

3 THE AUDITION

I actually couldn't believe I had been sacked, and to this day I will never know why. I was shell shocked, utterly demoralized and I didn't know what to do. One thing I did know was that I needed to get another job and quickly. I'd been given a term's notice so I began to apply to every school within commuting distance. It wasn't possible for me to teach at a South African government school as my UK teaching qualifications weren't recognized, so it had to be a private school and there were not nearly as many of those.

I battled to find employment and while I was still in panic mode, one of those chance remarks made in the staff room was to change everything in the long term and radically alter my whole future.

I remember as a small child, listening to BBC Radio 4 in the mornings as I got ready for school. My favourite presenter was Colin Fish, he had such a nice, sexy voice and he told the listeners lots of interesting things. As fate would have it, he'd married a lady from South Africa and moved over to live in Johannesburg. As soon as he stepped off the plane at Jan Smuts Airport, the South African Broadcasting Corporation (SABC), were waiting for him at the bottom of the steps, snapped him up, herded him into their main studios in Auckland Park and gave him the evening news to read.

The SABC staff reckoned they had a real prize here, a

bona fide BBC presenter, and they didn't come much better than that. What they had not bargained for was that no one had thought to brief him on local pronunciation and his first broadcast was a classic. Among the names in his debut news show were PW Botha, Mynie Grove and Vryheid. He pronounced all of them incorrectly. *Bota* for *Booerta*, Grove for *Hrowveer*, and *Vryheed* for *Vrayhate*.

I'm not sure how long he was employed in the news department, but he swiftly became a senior drama producer in the SABC and was a well-known and much loved figure.

His wife, Elizabeth Hamilton, was a leading actress in Johannesburg and a part time drama teacher at the school where I worked. I had previously mentioned to her, in a casual conversation one day that I had worked on radio in Libya, so she came up with the bright idea of me going for an audition at the SABC as a continuity announcer. For the first time I learned this was the correct title for writing and reading the links between programmes, I thought it sounded very professional! So, it was only years later, I realized I had been a continuity announcer. Wow, that sounded good didn't it?

I took a drive a few days later into town and slowly cruised past the broadcasting studios. There were two blocks of buildings and they soared several storeys high, surrounded by lots of security, and were quite frankly more than a little intimidating. No, I did not have the courage to apply to work there. It was one thing to sit in a two bit studio in Benghazi, with an audience of a couple of thousand friendly expats, but here I was looking at the national broadcaster of the most advanced country on the whole of the African continent.

I drove home.

"I've fixed up your audition," Elizabeth told me the following week. "Next Wednesday afternoon. They will give you time off from school and you drive to Auckland Park and take the entrance to the Radio Block."

I was petrified. Yes, I would love to work in radio again, it was like a dream come true. But I was not sure how I'd cope with the children if I had a full time job in Johannesburg, when we lived several miles away, closer to Pretoria. Now, there was no way I could turn down the appointment, no way that I could get out of it gracefully.

With my heart in my mouth I drove up to the car park entrance on Henley Road the following week. At first they refused to let me in. The guard on the gate shook his head when I said I was there for an audition, then reluctantly disappeared into his hut and re-appeared with a clipboard. Since he only spoke Afrikaans, we had a bit of a problem with names, but finally he found mine listed right at the bottom of the page and lifted the barrier.

It was quite a walk across another car park to reach the huge metal doors which led into the building. Urban legend had it that the studios were bomb proofed and would act as a refuge for the government should things go horribly wrong, and there was an all out revolution. I've no idea if this was true, but the huge, thick, outer metal doors gave you the impression that this could well be the case.

I presented myself at the reception desk, and after a few minutes I was escorted to a room somewhere and given a questionnaire to complete. Well that's what *they* called it. To me it looked more like an exam paper. The first part was easy, information about myself and I knew all that of course, but then came the difficult bit.

Who was Mynie Grove? I hadn't a clue, but rather than leave it blank, I wrote that she was in the government.

In what province is Pofadder? Where? I'd never heard of the place.

Who was the Prime Minister who preceded PW Botha? I hadn't a clue.

30

Doggedly I worked my way down a long, long list of questions, and I now know that I got every single one wrong, except the stuff about myself of course and they couldn't give me zero marks for that part.

The next paper asked me to write an introduction to a classical concert featuring an orchestral work by Handel. In those days I was quite a philistine - I'd never once tuned in to BBC Radio 3 in the UK to listen to classical music, and I had no idea how this was done. So I made it up. I *knew* that Handel had been the court musician for one of the King Georges (he wasn't), so I wrote that he *was*, and got all that horribly wrong as well. I made up stuff about his life which I hoped was vaguely close to the truth. Maybe they wouldn't notice or expect it to be accurate? I also gave Handel credit for dozens of other great musical works written by other composers, and I'm sure he's still turning in his grave as I write.

I was then asked to compose a five hundred word report on any topic. My imagination failed me, and all I could think of was a report on a fashion show. As I knew even less about fashion than I did about classical music, that was pretty abysmal as well. It was tricky to continually praise every outfit, but if you criticised any of them then you just sounded bitchy.

Blissfully unaware of how badly I had done, I was then taken down to the studios. There were dozens of them, at least that is how I remember it, and I was very impressed. The atmosphere resembled that of a convent, quiet and peaceful, as our footsteps made a slight whisper over the carpet-tiled floor. There were a few quiet murmurs from behind closed doors and lights above each one, red or green to tell everyone passing by, if they were live on air or you could enter safely.

Once in the studio, I was back in familiar surroundings, only this time the microphone was fixed to the desk, the chair didn't have stuffing coming out of the seat and the headphones were vastly superior to those I'd used in Benghazi. Again, there was a glass wall behind which sat an engineer who smiled and waved. I began to relax a little.

They gave me several sheets of paper and once the engineer had tested the sound levels after me reciting 'Mary had a Little Lamb', it was time for me to show what a wonderful presenter I would make.

As an aside here, I have no idea who first thought of using that particular nursery rhyme as a sound test, but it crops up time and time again. Sadly I have to admit, it was never the original version. There are some quite hair-raising versions, so don't ever ask what Mary did with her little lamb, or what sort of relationship they had. You don't want to know.

Back to my terrible audition. The first sheet I was to read in the studio was a list of international place names and Rio de Janeiro and Valparaiso and so on didn't faze me. I stumbled a bit over the township names such as Soshanguve, Thabazimbi and Vanderbijlpark, but I got through them as best as I could.

I turned over to the next page and froze. There in front of me was a whole page of Afrikaans. I was supposed to read this? In Afrikaans? I'd only been in South Africa for six months and had yet to learn more than five words of the language, and over twenty years later, I would shamefully admit to not having progressed much further.

For a moment I wondered if I should leave, and then thought, well, I have to do something. So taking a deep breath, I read slowly and phonetically each word on the page. Out of the corner of my eye I noticed movement on the other side of the glass wall, and glancing up, I saw the sound engineer had tears rolling down his cheeks. He was laughing so hard he fell off his chair. Manfully I ploughed on. When I next looked up I noticed that the control room was packed full of people, all holding their stomachs and killing themselves laughing.

While they might have thought my performance was hilarious, I was not so composed. This was all going very badly indeed.

They were still giggling as they escorted me from the studio and dumped me unceremoniously back outside the main entrance doors. It didn't help that a couple of other candidates walked out past me all smiles and confidence, chattering away in Afrikaans.

I should mention here at that time in 1983, the SABC was a bastion of male Afrikanerdom. They did broadcast a few programmes in English, and there was also the commercial channel Springbok Radio, that I'd listened to in Botswana which was partly in English, but the majority of both radio and television was in Afrikaans.

I drove home feeling very depressed. My future in radio had been dealt a resounding death blow, so I was not surprised when I received a letter a week later to say that I had failed my audition, but I might like to apply to the English Radio Drama Department. The letter was signed by Colin Fish.

In a sudden fit of desperation, I phoned the SABC, requested an audition, and then forgot all about it as I continued my frantic search for another teaching job. Months went by, I applied for and was accepted for a teaching post in Pretoria, and we moved house again.

I was therefore amazed to pick up a letter in the post box with the smart red and blue SABC logo in the top left hand corner. It invited me to an audition for the English Radio Drama Department the following day. I was to prepare three pieces to read on air and I was to present myself there at 10.30 in the morning.

Now I was in a total panic. Luckily it was during the school holidays and I was free to go, if I could find the courage and the material.

I raced over to the bookshelves. Shakespeare? No, I couldn't possibly massacre any of the Bard's great literary works, although it could be my revenge for what he put me through at school, hours of studying plays I barely understood. The rest of the shelves contained popular works of fiction and were not at all suitable. I could hardly dramatize Harold Robbins or Dennis Wheatley, I only had sixteen hours to come up with something and I would also need to catch a bit of sleep in that time.

I had only appeared on stage once, in Libya. We had been active members of the secret, underground, amateur dramatic society. Secret, because such activities were banned under Islamic law, so we rehearsed in private houses, and used the British School hall for performances. I've been told that our standards were exceptionally high, and my ex-husband was a leading light in many of our productions. (As he is now my ex-husband, I shall refer to him as my ex to avoid any confusion with my second, adorable husband).

So, I was always earmarked as Stage Manager, or Props or anything that involved organization, and I'm sure that I was only offered that part once as a sort of thank you for all my hard work, and for housing all the play scripts in one of our spare rooms.

I'm certainly no actress. My first and last stage debut was the shrinking violet that had apparently been chased across the park in 'Big Bad Mouse', the role that Jimmy Edwards made so famous many years earlier.

I was dressed up in a tweed skirt, shapeless cardigan and clumpy lace-up shoes, with my hair scraped back in a bun, and the only comment I ever received was from one lady on the beach, who exclaimed that I looked so much better on stage than I did in real life. Yes, she really thought I looked

34

better in my stage clothes than the skimpy bikini from a Harrods' sale I was so proud of. I was not impressed with my performance, and quite obviously neither was the audience.

Now I was faced with the dilemma of approaching the microphone the following day and I hadn't one script, let alone three. I'm hopeless at accents, I do so admire those people who, at the drop of a hat can mimic regional variations, but maybe I could get away with an Irish one? I had spent the first ten years of my life in Dublin after all. And how about a child? Yes, just pitch my voice a little higher and that might work, and a straight dramatic piece to make up the three.

Now I'd worked out what I could possibly do at a pinch, but where was I going to find any suitable material?

I raided the children's books, but that failed to yield anything so, in desperation, I sat down to write my own scripts. For the Irish accent I composed a one sided conversation about an IRA boyfriend who was about to get arrested. For the child, a telephone conversation about how the little brat was successfully playing one parent off against another to go on a skiing trip, and the last one was a short piece on modern teenage children from a very harassed parent. I went over and over them again and again, even as I was driving into Auckland Park the next day.

Once again I was escorted down to the studios and into a room, where I noticed with horror there was no table. I was expected to *stand* in front of the microphone and do the audition. This was a first. Usually I had my scripts on a table and looked down as I read, and now I would have to find a way of holding the papers in front of me without obscuring the microphone. The problem was I had not written them in very large letters (learning curve number one) and it was going to be a nightmare to see the words.

Besides the sound controller, there was another man behind the glass who introduced himself as Jack Mullen. He looked important, but I had no idea what role he played at the SABC. I was incredibly nervous as I stepped up to the microphone with the script quivering in my hand stretched out to the other side of it. It didn't help that the mike had an 'anti-pop' shield, a large, black circular net to help cut out the popping and hissing sounds that so often occur when you say the letters 'p' or 's.'

Once I started, I began to relax and managed to get through all three scripts, remembering just in time to put on the right voice to match the right parts. When I reached the end, I stopped to look up into the control room. I was aware that any work they might offer me was not going to be full time, so that took some of the pressure off. I didn't think I had made a total fool of myself, but I knew they were not gasping in admiration either.

"You have worked on radio before?" Jack asked.

"Yes, in Benghazi, in Libya. 'You are tuned to the broadcasting service of the Libyan Arab Jamahriya, in the English language on 904.3 FM'," I repeated like a parrot.

"Tell me some more of your background. What experience have you had in drama?"

If the truth were told, none whatsoever. You couldn't count those few lines in an amateur production six years ago, but I was not about to tell him that. My mind went into overtime and raced even further back through the years.

"I first appeared on stage at the Gaiety Theatre in Dublin at the age of three..." I began.

"Really!" exclaimed Jack. "I was there too, so you are also from Dublin?"

I was happy to agree I was and had lived there for ten years. What I didn't add was that yes, I *had* been on stage, but only in the very back row of a ballet performance, the annual show put on by the very posh dancing school I was dragged to every Saturday morning. And all the pupils were involved, had they been left out, the fee paying parents would have thrown all their toys out of the cot and taken to the streets with placards. Hopefully I would not have to explain this, but Jack was happily reminiscing.

Then came the words I did not want to hear.

"Where did you get your material?"

Reluctantly, I said I had written it myself, because I'd only found out yesterday about the audition, and there hadn't been time to go to the library and find some proper plays. There was a long, very long, pregnant silence. I wanted to shrivel up and die, I should never have come, what a big mistake this was.

"Hmmm, well I'll use you," Jack said at last, "not that you're any great shakes as an actress..." He wasn't telling me anything I didn't know already.

"... but," he continued, "you *can* write. So, go home and write."

For a few moments I stood there transfixed. I didn't walk out of the studio, I floated back to the car. An important producer at the head office of a national broadcasting corporation told me I could write. Me! After all these years! I could do it!

Well... maybe. There was just a little thing such as earning a living that was going to get in the way. There were household bills to pay, and stuff for the children, and petrol and so on and so on. My ex had changed his job yet again so we could not depend on his income.

I could solve this by working longer hours, fine, but what was I going to write? And who was I going to write for? And, who would pay me to write? I would make a plan, I promised myself. But the thought was far easier than the deed.

I decided the first problem to solve was the 'who,' but the decision was taken out of my hands a few days later when

Elizabeth Hamilton bounced into the staff room at school and thrust a piece of paper and a booklet into my hand. It was entitled "English Service, Radio Drama – the Writing of Plays for Radio (A brief guide)."

"I hear that Jack Mullen was very impressed with you," she told me, much to my delight. "Now, there is a play writing competition which you *must* enter and I've snaffled this booklet to help you write it in the correct format. You had better get going though, as the closing date is next week."

"Goodness!" I gulped. "How long does the play have to be?"

"An hour," Elizabeth replied. "Probably about seventy odd pages, oh, and it must be typed. Do you have a typewriter?"

No, I didn't, but I would make a plan. It was something I hadn't even thought of. Of course you couldn't submit handwritten articles to anyone, so a typewriter was essential. If I was hoping to make any money by writing, I would first have to find the capital to purchase the basic necessities, plus of course the paper.

On the way home, I wondered how I could ever afford a typewriter. I had no idea how much they cost, but when I mentioned this to my ex that night, he said not to worry, he would sort it out.

He did, for when he came home from work the following day, under one arm was a shiny, blue Remington something-or-other, complete with a correctable ribbon. It wasn't new, for apart from a few small dents and scratches, the letter 'n' was missing. Never one to let a small problem get in the way of a great author, he suggested that I could insert them by hand for the moment, while he tried to sort out where we could buy one.

I wasn't sure if he meant a new typewriter or a new letter 'n', but I didn't like to ask.

Meanwhile, I had scoured the newspapers and discovered

that typewriters were not cheap. I resolved to make do with what had fallen mysteriously out of somewhere, and was now residing on a chair in the television room. It was never wise to question my ex too closely about certain matters, and I had learned to turn a blind eye for the sake of peace.

The dining room table would become my office and, putting three cushions underneath me and inserting the first piece of paper between the rollers, I was ready to start.

First, although I had lots of ideas for my play, I figured I should read the booklet to show me how to do it. This small brochure had been put together as a guide by someone at the SABC, and was absolutely hilarious. Through all my subsequent travels, I still have it today.

It contained a couple of gems of 'what not to do' like the following:

For a radio script, dialogue is always written in lower case and the directions in capitals.

FX: [SOUND EFFECTS] A LETTER IS DROPPED THROUGH THE LETTER BOX.

Can you really get this message across with sound only? If you don't think so you could add the following.

JOHN: Postman's early!

MARY: How do you know that?

JOHN: [MOVING OFF TO DOOR] Because, my dear girl, a letter just dropped through the letter box. Elementary my dear Watson!

Rather contrived and certainly clumsy.

They gave another example of how NOT to write for radio.

FX: JOHN TIPTOES DOWN THE CARPETED STAIRS. QUIETLY HE OPENS THE LIVING ROOM DOOR. HE TIPTOES OFF MIKE, TAKES A 16TH CENTURY HALBERD FROM THE WALL AND TIPTOES ON TO MIKE AGAIN. ON MIKE, WE HEAR HIM

BREATHING, AND THEN WITH AN ALMOST ANIMAL LIKE ROAR, HE RAISES THE HALBERD AND SWINGS IT DOWN VIOLENTLY, SMASHING THE TELEVISION SET.

I giggled when I read that, because none of it makes sense if you're trying to tell a story only with sound! How do you know John is tiptoeing downstairs, grabbing weapons and then destroying the TV? We can only hear his breathing and roaring. He could be lion taming, or climbing Mount Everest as far as the listener is concerned, or even breaking into the back of the supermarket.

So there is a certain technique in writing for radio, and later I learned to think in sound, but for my first attempt, I struggled.

Seventy-odd pages seemed a lot to write, far more than I'd ever written before. Full of enthusiasm, I rose at 5am the following morning and began. It took a lot more pressure than I had expected to press down the typewriter keys, and after an hour of thumping, swearing and ripping numerous pieces of precious paper out of the rollers, I admitted defeat. Perhaps, if I wrote it by hand, then I could copy it later.

Of course by 6am I had to stop. It was time to get the children up for school, and then drive myself to a different school for a day's teaching. There were also the usual household tasks to get done and meals to prepare, and I was exhausted by the end of the day, but that was a small price to pay. I decided if I was going to get this done, I must learn to make sacrifices.

So while the rest of the family slept peacefully, I laboured away, writing two sentences, scratching out one of them, stopping to remember who was on and off mike, and who was where and what they were supposed to be doing.

I realized I had written that one character was having a bath, and then I had her joining in the group discussion. No, I couldn't put everyone in the bathroom as she lay naked in the tub, so it was back to the drawing board.

It dawned on me, there was a lot more planning I hadn't done, or even thought about. If you send someone off to town and they suddenly pipe up with a comment, you are going to confuse everyone and probably yourself as well. Although I had been told I *could* write, no one had ever told me *how* to write in a structured way. The booklet helped, but it didn't cover everything.

I hit on the idea of making a small cut out of each character, and as I sent them here there and everywhere, I placed them physically where they were supposed to be.

I laboured all weekend at the play, being totally anti-social with the family, assuring them they would have my complete and undivided attention the following weekend.

By Sunday night I had finished it and now all that was left to do was to type it up. This was a mission in itself, remember the missing 'n'? I was up most of the night on Tuesday, and by Wednesday morning it was ready to go. I took time to read it through, and then I got cold feet. There was no way I could send this in for a national competition, it just wasn't good enough. Well, maybe the story was not too bad, but the presentation...?

Before leaving for school, I dumped the whole manuscript in the rubbish bin and decided to stick to teaching. I was not cut out to be a writer, it was hard enough as my thoughts flew a lot faster than my hands could write, and then all this fiddling about on the paper, making corrections or finding just the right word which had previously escaped me. It was never going to happen.

4 WHAT CAN I WRITE?

I forgot all about the competition, avoiding Elizabeth Hamilton as much as possible. I didn't look forward to telling her I had not entered, especially after she had gone to so much trouble on my behalf, so when the second letter bearing the SABC logo arrived, I opened it and gave it a quick glance, and then read it again and again and again.

I had won! Yes, my play was judged the best! 'The Dead Cert' had come first-equal with another play by a well-known writer. And that wasn't all. They were going to produce it, and it would be broadcast to the whole of South Africa - to over thirty-five million people!

Well, I guess that is a bit of an exaggeration as over thirty million of them didn't speak or understand English, but it does sound good on paper, doesn't it? And they could listen in if they wanted to, even if they didn't understand a word of it.

I rushed to tell the family, who were suitably unimpressed, though they did cheer up when they saw me waving the enclosed cheque for a thousand Rand. That was more than I earned for six weeks' teaching.

Then it dawned on me. The last time I saw my play was on the top of the rubbish bin. My ex smiled in a particularly smug way, and admitted that after scraping the spaghetti and the tea bags off it, he had taken it by hand to the SABC. I gave him an enormous hug.

I was now hooked, and from that moment on there was no going back. My first effort ever and it had won! I walked on air for days.

I wanted to frame the cheque and was loath to cash it, but that would have been really silly. Although I've had a good, long think, I cannot remember what I spent it on. I suspect it was used to pay off household bills, and I probably took everyone out for a steak dinner. South Africa has the best steaks in the world.

So, what could I write next? I scoured the papers and discovered that the English Language Radio Service broadcast a fifteen minute story every morning, and there were two plays broadcast twice a week in the evenings as well. I could supply *all* of those, couldn't I?

A few days later I sat down to write my first short story, about a fish eagle that got shot by a farmer and left for dead. We knew he was a bad man because he wouldn't let his aspiring and talented young son play the violin as it was a sissy occupation. Since the nasty farmer got eaten alive at the end by the wounded bird, it was not exactly a cheerful subject, but I popped it in an envelope and sent it in to the SABC by mail.

I had a phone call a few days later. Would I like to come in to the studios and record the morning story? I was thrilled, and to celebrate the occasion my ex bought me my first briefcase to help create the image of a successful writer.

Once again I was conducted down to the studios and settled myself comfortably behind the microphone. I had practiced reading my story over and over again and was satisfied that I had got all the pauses in the right places, with just enough hype for the cliff-hangers and the exciting bits.

To my horror, they brought in a different script. This was *someone else's* story they wanted me to read. What had happened to mine? For the moment I said nothing and skimmed through the script while I waited for the sound engineer to stop fiddling in the control room. I remember thinking, not very modestly, that this story was not as good as mine, and I did not find it particularly easy to read. However, after only a few fluffs and re-takes it was over, and the producer Ralf Lawson, came into the studio to say he was happy with the recording.

I plucked up my courage and asked him if they'd received my story by any chance?

Yes, they had.

And were they going to use it?

Yes, in a month or so. The cheque would be posted fourteen days after broadcast.

I raced home and in between teaching, looking after the family, preparation for school and other household tasks, I scribbled away at every opportunity. I must add here, like nearly all households, we had a maid during the week, who cleaned the house and did the washing and the ironing. Had that not been the case, I would never have had a spare moment to write and my life would have been totally different.

While teaching at the posh school - yes, the lot who sacked me - I had a class of young children aged around seven, and at the end of each day I always told them a story. I'd told stories at home to my own two children about a character I invented called Horatio Tumbletum, and these had gone down quite well with my very discerning offspring, so I thought I would try them out in the classroom.

Much to my amazement, they proved popular, but then I have to admit, he was an engaging little creature, small, very furry and cuddly, with long arms and very short legs. He'd come from outer space and had an extremely loud voice and was very rude to grownups, my young audience loved that. He changed colour according to his mood, ate the dust and rubbish from the vacuum cleaner and was a whizz at mending anything.

So, nothing daunted, I submitted one of the stories to the SABC for the children's programme and much to my delight, they accepted it. When the time for broadcast arrived I sat breathlessly next to the radio. The children disappeared out into the garden while I sat spellbound, but it was only as they mentioned the credits that I thought of recording it. It was too late now.

I sat down to put another one on paper. That too was accepted for broadcast, and I picked up my pen again. Then I paused. Wait, if I gave all my Horatio stories away, maybe it was *not* such a good idea. Already in my mind I could see every shop stuffed full of Horatio toothbrushes, Horatio cushions, Horatio babies with diapers, Horatio mugs, Horatio pencils and pencil boxes, Horatio carrying a small vacuum cleaner... I'm sure you get the picture.

I also reasoned it would make an excellent mood toy for young couples to give each other. If you received a version of him in red, then you knew the giver was angry with you, green meant jealousy and so on. I could clearly see the millions rolling in. So, no more Horatio for the SABC. I would write a whole book.

Hey, this writing lark was a piece of cake! I mentally ordered the yacht with a built in office on the aft deck as we cruised gently across the ocean.

For my next children's story, I would make up something quite different, I think it was a story about a boy who was given a drum for his birthday.

Even with my unbounded optimism, I realized it was going to take a few months before I put in the order for the ocean cruiser, and as the SABC were paying scriptwriters by the broadcast minute, I reckoned I should churn out a few more sixty minute plays.

I had little knowledge of South Africa as a whole and little idea about her history except for the apartheid story. This I found puzzling, as there seemed to be little evidence of it. Yes, there was separate transport for blacks and whites, and different entrances into the bottle stores, but as far as I could see, those were the only signs. There were plenty of black Africans everywhere you went.

So for my next masterpiece I wrote about a more familiar scene and set it in no man's land, featuring two families competing for the largest marrow prize at the local produce show. I had no idea if such events were even held in South Africa, but I went ahead regardless. This too was accepted, and my next trip into Auckland Park was by invitation to sit in on the recording of 'The Dead Cert', which I had written for the competition.

As I was introduced to the cast, I attempted to appear as nonchalant as possible and not let my mouth drop open too far. Wow! These were people I had seen on television, right in my TV lounge, and now they were going to say the words that I had written for them. I had to pinch myself to make sure I was alive and really there.

I sat in a side room with the cast and watched as the actors stepped up to the mike, and an engineer made various noises using boxes of gravel for footsteps, and opened and closed doors using just a block of wood attached to the lock. I saw how the actors began speaking a little way off the mike and came closer to give the impression they had just arrived, and how they were stopped now and again to repeat their lines the way the producer wanted them read.

I was also privy to the idle chatter of the cast who were waiting for their scenes to be recorded, eavesdropping on the titbits of media life. I especially remember one of the actors was having a row with his agent who wanted him to do a commercial for a hair remover, which would show him covered in bright pink cream before appearing bald. He was adamant that no amount of money would persuade him to appear on national TV with no hair. It simply wasn't fashionable in those days!

A few weeks later, I received a phone call to tell me the play was going to be broadcast the following Friday, and I rushed out to buy an audio cassette tape. I was going to listen to it, and then keep it for posterity, maybe listen again when I was in my rocking chair in the old folks' home. But I came up against strong opposition.

"You promised we could go to the drive-in on Friday night!"

"Yes, I know, but we can go on Saturday night instead, I want to listen to my play and record it at the same time."

"Then why can't you just put the tape in and leave it running?"

"Two reasons. Firstly, the play doesn't come on until eight o'clock and the drive-in starts at half past seven. And I could only buy a ninety minute tape, that's the longest they make, so I need to be here to turn it over half way through. As it is, I'll miss a couple of sentences while I fiddle about."

No one was convinced, but I stood my ground and to this day I can't remember if they all went off without me, or sat and sulked and refused to listen. I did record the play and vowed to keep it forever, but today I have no idea where it is, and I've nothing left to play an audio tape on any more. I do still have the paper version though, printed out by the SABC, with all the letter 'n's in place, thank goodness. They must have got someone to re-type it.

I never got to hear either the morning story I broadcast, or the one I had written, recorded by someone else, as I was teaching at school when it was on the air, and I didn't have the courage to take a radio into the classroom and tune in.

It was at that point I realized I was never going to get big-headed about my writing. If the family were unimpressed, then no one outside the family was going to be impressed either. I'm also quite a shy person, and while everyone at the weekend *braai* (barbeque) was talking about politics, the weather or how the kids were doing, there never seemed to be an opening when I could announce "Did you know I had become a writer?"

In time, the cheque for my morning story arrived in the post and I raced down to the post office and opened a savings account. In no time at all I would amass a small fortune and start living the high life.

What was I thinking?

I'm sure the producers, Jack Mullen and Ralf Lawson, began to regret giving me any encouragement at all, as I then bombarded them with stories and plays, one after the other. Some were accepted, most rejected.

Jack was very kind and always wrote back with a critique and I remember one letter in which he expressed his exasperation, reminding me that a cast the size of Ben Hur was beyond the financial resources of the SABC for one radio play. On another occasion, he pointed out that I did not give any motivation whatsoever, for the heroine teacher to climb a hundred foot electric pylon, to rescue the pupil who had murdered her father with a broken milk bottle the night before. He really did have a point there.

Jack also mentioned in another rejection letter there *were* other scriptwriters in South Africa, and as we all had a different style, they would have to spread the work around a little.

I was in such a hurry to join the Monte Carlo set before I got too old and ugly, that I had begun to toss off manuscripts with little or no thought.

Reasoning that the BBC would have a larger budget, nothing daunted, I then began posting off all the stuff the SABC didn't want to the British Broadcasting Corporation, but they were not impressed with my efforts either. They said some very nice things in their rejection letters, but since Auckland Park didn't want them, I wasn't too surprised when they all came back from London.

I even bombarded the Zimbabwean Broadcasting Company, but they simply sent me a letter on recycled paper saying they couldn't afford to pay any money for plays, or anything else for that matter.

Just as I was beginning to despair, I received another call, this time from Timothy Bungay who headed up Springbok Radio. The same station I'd listened to every night in Botswana.

I'd been particularly fascinated in the advertising breaks when they talked about a product called a Kreepy Krauly. Not understanding a word of it, I assumed it was an anti-insect spray. It was only years later when I discovered that Kreepy Kraulys were automated swimming pool cleaners, invented and manufactured in South Africa.

"I understand you've spent time in Libya," Timothy Bungay said over the phone.

"Yes, we were there for five and a half years."

"So you must have some interesting stories of what it was like to live in an Arab country?"

"Goodness yes, it was amazing. Brewing our own beer, the secret theatre group, the Morality Police parked outside our villas, and my dogs were shot, right in our front garden. That was awful."

"I thought it would sound interesting. Would you be willing to write a series of talks for Springbok Radio? Each one should be fifteen minutes long and feature a different aspect."

Is the Pope Catholic? Well I didn't actually say that to Timothy, but I was over the moon. To be *asked* to write for broadcast was so much more important than sending scripts in on spec hoping they'd be accepted. This time I knew they were going to pay me before I even picked up a pen! I accepted with alacrity, but there was one thing I had to do first.

49

I went to the post office, withdrew my hard earned money and went out to buy myself a typewriter, one that had all twenty six letters of the alphabet. This was now the real deal and it was about time I began to look and act like a professional writer.

I found it very easy to write about our antics in Benghazi. I could recall with humour the night of the bayonets at the radio station, the illegal drinking and the quirks of shopping and entertaining. Much to my surprise, Timothy was pleased with what I sent him, and added to my euphoria by asking me to come in to the studios and record them myself. I would get even more money for doing that.

It took several sessions to lay all ten of the programmes down to tape and I had a great time in the studio doing it. I was feeling quite familiar with the SABC by this time - even the guard on the car park gate smiled and waved me through without any fuss.

Again, I never heard those programmes on air, as they went out in the morning after the new term had started and I was back in the classroom, teaching yet another version of 'The Great Trek', which turned up year after year after year on the history syllabus. But the cheque duly arrived in the post, so who was I to complain?

Having finally got the message that there were other writers out there who contributed to the SABC's programme schedules, I cast about for other outlets. What about women's magazines? I'd never bought any, I preferred to read books and I didn't like looking at those gorgeous women I was supposed to emulate. No way! So, a little research was in order.

Off I went to CNA, which in South Africa is the equivalent of WHSmith in the UK. They had a policy of allowing people to browse through their books and magazines for as long as they liked, so I didn't actually buy any of them, but ducked down behind the shelves and after flicking through each one, I scribbled down the addresses for contributions. I had never noticed before that most weekly publications were happy to consider stories and articles sent in by the public.

I began to bombard them with equal fervour. I wrote about Libya, just in case they had missed the broadcasts. I wrote about the time we broke down in the game park and I thought my last hours had come, and our other adventures in Kenya and all about the riding school in Botswana.

Woman's Value was the publication that particularly liked my stuff, and they printed several of my articles - not all, but a fair few. I am trying now to remember the names of the other magazines that were happy to send me cheques for my efforts. I think one was called Femina, but my memory is not as good as it was, which is why I must quickly finish this book and the next one before I forget who I am!

I do remember Cosmopolitan accepting one story, and they wrote and asked me to send in a picture of myself to use on the page. I sent them one I'd had taken at the Lion Park in Johannesburg, holding two lion cubs, but begged them to return it after use, as they had promised in their letter. I never saw it again, and those were the only lion cubs I have ever cuddled. I've never quite forgiven them for that.

When I'd run out of life stories, I began to write short, funny articles, on such topics as 'How to Keep your Man', and 'How to do the Weekly Budget', and 'How to Pack for a Weekend Away for Four in Fifteen Minutes Flat', all very tongue in cheek.

In those days the centre of the magazine industry was located in Durban and Cape Town, both miles away from Johannesburg, so all correspondence was by post or snail mail, as we call it today. So it took a long time between submissions, acceptance and publication three months later, but eventually the cheques dropped into the post box in Irene,

51

our local village, along with a free copy of the magazine.

However, the paper publications did not pay as well as the national broadcaster, and other household expenses nibbled their way into the payments. I could see my yacht sailing off into the distance without me. So, at the beginning of the next term I returned to the classroom.

Sadly, in December 1985 Springbok Radio was closed down. It was a big blow not only to me as a contributor, but to the hundreds of thousands of listeners the length and breadth of South Africa. One day shortly after the announcement, when I delivered yet another play to Timothy Bungay, he took me into one of the vacant offices and showed me stacks and stacks of mail bags, all bulging with letters begging those at top management levels not to close down their beloved radio station. It was to no avail. Once the hierarchy had made up their minds there was no changing them.

So it looked as if my brief foray in the writing world was going to be severely pruned. Springbok had accepted several of my plays and in the last year, Jack Mullen had only called me in a couple of times to act in a radio play. He had dozens of much better people to choose from, and frankly, I will never be much of an actress. I go as far as most teachers do in classrooms the world over, as we attempt to make our lessons exciting, thrilling and appetizing, to a captive audience who is not there by choice, and who decided even before entering the classroom, that today was going to be yet another great, big bore.

And that wasn't the point. I wanted to write, not act. I was beginning to get strange sort of withdrawal symptoms when I wasn't writing or thinking up new plots and scenarios.

I was still searching around for more outlets to suffocate with my humble offerings, when I noticed a short piece in one of the local freebie newspapers that dropped through our door every Thursday. It was called 'Suider Beeld', and it was all in Afrikaans, except this one letter to the editor which was written in English.

I had a brainwave. I would write to the editor and suggest that maybe one article a week could be written in English, which might increase interest among the English speaking community, and provide practice for those who spoke Afrikaans at the same time.

They fell for it, and commissioned a weekly column of about a thousand words. The money they offered was more than acceptable and what was more, I would get paid regularly every week. They even arranged for a young man on a motorcycle to come either to school or the house every week and collect the copy. Did this make me a professional writer at last? I hesitated over that one. No, I think you have to actually earn your living to be a 'real professional'. I'd not got there yet.

5 DOWN TO GRASS ROOTS

I had fun writing about local events, usually with a satirical slant, which I found out did not go down well with everyone.

Suider Beeld also requested a picture to grace the column, and as I sadly did not have one of me cuddling lion cubs any more, my ex took several dozen with our camera. He is an excellent photographer, but I do not have either a pretty or a photogenic face, and he struggled to come up with anything that looked vaguely human!

In later months I regretted that photo. I should have sent them one of Marilyn Munroe, or possibly Goldie Hawn, because people began to recognize me in places such as the local supermarket and the post office.

I am not a 'front of house' sort of person, and people would rush up to me and gush and say how much they loved my column. I would turn bright red, get very embarrassed and stand mumbling like some speechless idiot, while the children looked at me curiously and ask me what was wrong. I was never sure what to say, even though I was always asked the same questions.

"Where do you get your ideas?"

"How do you think of things?"

"I've always wanted to write in the newspaper, will you teach me how?"

That was on the plus side, but there were other people who were positively aggressive.

"How dare you criticize our mayor like that?"

"Don't you know that road is going to be developed later?"

"How can you say that dogs shouldn't be left in the car when I go shopping?"

"Who are you to tell me what to do?"

I wasn't sure what to say to this group of people either. Many times I was backed up against the frozen food counter freezing my rear end against plastic bags of peas or carrots, while some unhappy reader explained why I had got it all wrong.

I tried to bleat that it was all in fun, tongue in cheek and so on, but they were not prepared to listen. I took to doing the weekly shop, with the children's help, at super high speed. I wrote 'How to Train Your Children to Help you do the Weekly Shopping in Four Minutes', which was published in *Woman's Value*, earning me a few more of those precious Rand.

I also began to understand why those really famous people in Hollywood attacked the paparazzi and broke their cameras along with any limb they could reach. If this was the treatment one could expect by being a very unimportant writer in a free newspaper, how much worse must it be for them?

At that point in my life I decided that I was a 'behind the scenes sort of person', and I would never again seek the limelight. Even today, I have to take a very deep breath before a book signing.

Another article that earned me a few cents was the story of the cake my children won at their primary school fete. Now I never win anything. I'm convinced that if I bought all but one of the raffle tickets on offer, I would still be the one to go home empty handed. As kids do, they pestered me for money so they could buy raffle tickets for this amazing cake and then present it to me as their gift to Mummy. That's the way kids' minds work.

To my amazement, they actually won this huge cake covered in bright turquoise icing with a couple of dozen plastic racing cars on the top.

I am hopeless at making cakes I've been known to completely ruin a foolproof Mary Baker packet mix, so I was quite pleased with my 'free' present, and cut slices for the children to put in their lunchboxes.

I cut more slices the following day, and the day after that and then the next day, and the subsequent day and still the cake didn't seem to get any smaller. In desperation I sliced it in half and put some in the freezer, for by now, the texture was closer to solid concrete than light, fluffy sponge. I had no idea how long cakes stayed fresh, normally they were consumed within a day in our house, but as I mentioned, this cake was big - very big!

Finally the children rebelled, and it dawned on me that if I persisted with the lunchbox offerings, the dental bills might be a lot higher than a few slices of 'free' cake. With a sigh of relief, I tipped the remaining slices into the bin, racing cars and all.

On the positive side, the article appeared in one of the magazines a few months later and I hoped they might offer me the weekly back page comedy slot. There was just the faint possibility that the regular contributor might fall down a manhole or emigrate to Alaska or somewhere similar, and I would be there waiting breathlessly in the wings. It never happened and I realize now it was probably written by the in-house staff themselves. Using a 'pen name' had never occurred to me.

I remembered my earlier admiration of Jo, from 'Little Women', I felt I was really following in her footsteps and wondered if Louisa May Alcott had based the book on a real family. I must get round to Googling it one day.

While many people were amazed that I'd got a foot in the door at the SABC, known for its male Afrikaner dominance, I had an even more surprising phone call one day from one of the Afrikaans-speaking producers in the Radio Education Department. Would I please come in and see him about a possible series for Black Radio?

Now radio has always been an important medium for informal education, and also for propaganda. The SABC had several satellite stations spread throughout the country, each broadcasting in a different African language; I think there are nine in all. Certainly today South Africa has eleven official languages, English and Afrikaans being only two of them.

This time I floated into the SABC and was soon ensconced in a bright, cheerful office sitting opposite the top producer for the Informal Education Department for the Black Radio Services. Johann was a pleasant, friendly guy, tall, thin and very, very Afrikaans. He was simply charming, polite, and like many Afrikaans men, he behaved toward women as men had done in Victorian days, with respect and courtesy.

He ordered coffee and told me he was considering commissioning a series on looking after animals, with the emphasis on cows, goats and chickens. It was entitled 'Health in Man and Animals'.

I knew as much about livestock as I did about the stock market, but I was not going to admit that now. While animals, especially cows, are very important to the Africans, they do not always take great care of them, so I was informed. Few were ever taken to the state vets who charged peanuts, or even treated the animals for free. The aims and objectives of this series would encourage the owners to treat their animals kindly and persuade them to seek professional advice.

He wanted thirteen programmes altogether and he handed me a list of titles over the desk. Could I write these?

Probably not, I thought, and immediately answered "yes," with what I hoped was lots of confidence, holding my coffee cup in both hands as they quivered like aspen leaves. (I've never seen an aspen leaf, but I've read this description in other books by great authors, and it seems appropriate).

As soon as I got back home, I did a bit more aspen quivering. I had signed a contract. There it was in my new briefcase, a piece of blue paper with the smart SABC logo on the top commissioning me to write thirteen, fifteen minute episodes for radio. Looking at the date for delivery, I saw that I had three months to complete the job.

I did a quick bit of maths, never my strong suit, and realized that I would have to put in a lot of hours, and with the day to day activities that demanded my time, I would have to get up even earlier each morning. I would also have to do a lot of research on cows, chickens and goats. The nearest I had ever got to any of them was on little plastic trays covered with cling film in the supermarket. Let me amend that, no goat meat on the plastic trays.

Bearing in mind this was in pre-internet days, I hunted the local library for books on animal husbandry and was severely disappointed. There didn't appear to be much call for them in the middle of the city. No one I knew had a garden large enough to keep any animals that size. I was beginning to panic.

It was quite by chance I saw a display in our local shopping mall selling the Encyclopaedia Britannica. That was the answer, except the price for a set was astronomical.

"No problem," said the weaselly little man, whistling through the gap in his front teeth as he swept his hand through the greasy hair which surrounded his pimply face. "You can buy them on credit, look, only these few Rand every month."

I picked up the one marked 'C-D' and searched for chickens. There were pages and pages and pages of information about them. Goodness, if I learned all this I would qualify as a chicken veterinarian.

"Where do I sign?" I asked quickly before I could change

my mind.

"And, as an added bonus," the pimply youth added, "we will throw in a complete set of the Children's Encyclopaedias as well. That's right, sign here. And here. And here. Now, where shall we deliver them?"

I can't remember exactly how the books were packaged when they arrived at the door, but I do remember that I could not pick up more than four volumes at a time. We installed a bookcase in the television lounge, evicted the television into the day lounge, and my new, partly-paid for purchases took pride of place on the shelves, next to an old desk we'd rescued from the municipal dump. I had by now taken over the TV lounge entirely, and I thought the window, looking out onto a brick wall, was particularly suitable for a writer. No distractions.

True to the weaselly, pimply youth's word, the full set of encyclopaedias for adults was accompanied by the Children's Britannica, although I was a little uncomfortable to see each one was stamped as being a gift to the children of Namibia from a charitable organization. That couldn't be right surely? But when I flipped through the pages, I was relieved to see they had several sensible articles on chickens, goats and cows that even I could understand.

I quickly, easily and very successfully buried my guilty feeling about leaving the younger generation of Namibia in ignorance, as I put the twenty volumes on the shelves as well. I was going to help educate many thousands more over the radio using these books wasn't I?

I was ready to start.

In radio, long discussions with yourself are not encouraged. Shakespeare may have got away with long soliloquies, but that was not going to work for the SABC. If I used a presenter to explain how to recognize if your cow was

59

on its last legs, or your chickens had lost all their feathers, it was going to sound like a lecture in school, and I had a horrid feeling that any listeners would simply switch off.

The 'clunk, click' syndrome is well-known in the media. It's what happens when you don't enthral your audience in those first, few, vital seconds. Fail to do that and they click the remote and move on to the next station to see if there's anything better on another channel. Men are particularly good at this, hogging the remote control as if it was the Olympic torch, and flying through one offering after another, pausing only to watch a leering, half naked girl for fifteen milliseconds, before moving on through the next one hundred and forty other programmes currently on the air.

So, I needed at least two characters to talk to one another. I battled for several moments and wrote the first few exchanges, but even to me, they sounded lame and boring. Remembering my days in the classroom, I hit on the idea of creating a family, whose animals were perpetually sick, but who were persuaded to consult the vet who then became a great friend. By the end of the series my hero family would have the healthiest animals, producing the most milk, the strongest offspring, all culminating in winning the top prizes in the local agricultural fair. I'm sure you get the idea.

I decided to throw in a bit of humour as well, to make the series more entertaining, and hoped that a different culture would understand the funny bits, especially when they were translated into the nine African languages. I opened the notepad I had bought especially for the occasion, picked up my pen and began to write.

That first fifteen minute episode took me three days to compose. Once I had created the family in my head it went quite quickly and I was feeling pleased with myself, until I remembered that I had forgotten to really think about my characters. I had them all over the place, driving into town, visiting the shopping mall, and popping next door for a cup of tea. I had just taken them for a picnic at the weekend, when I realized with horror that I had transplanted them into a first world urban family, who just happened to keep cows, goats and chickens in the back garden.

I really couldn't believe I had been so stupid. I had to think like one of the family in my target audience, so I closed my eyes and went back in time to Botswana and the villages we rode through on the ponies. (That was back in the time I ran the 'worst riding school in the world', and is recounted in another book). I saw the women tending the mealie patch, the men sitting under the acacia trees, and the hot sun beating down on the dusty earth while the animals foraged in the rubbish dumps.

This was my target audience, not some pseudo town dwellers who owned cars and credit cards. I tore up my first efforts and began all over again. I had to keep this simple.

To be fair to Johann, he had given me a list of topics and a few notes to help me, but I was a bit puzzled by the line which simply said 'wash hands'.

Over the next two decades I would write unceasingly about the benefits of washing hands, after communing with nature, changing babies' nappies, petting animals and touching livestock, before preparing food, and before you put your hands near your face, or handled small children. This was all second nature to anyone brought up with an indoor bathroom and running water in the kitchen, but not so obvious to rural peasants. The people living outside the towns and cities had to fetch their water, sometimes from miles away, and water is heavy! If you don't believe me just fill a jerry can to the brim and try and balance that on your head!

So, while I was going to urge people to keep their hands clean, I also had to bear in mind that I was not to overdo it, as another thought had struck me. I could of course explain that germs carry diseases and these diseases make you sick, but how was I going to convince my audience? You can't see germs on your hands and you have no proof that something unseen is going to make you ill. Was this another ploy by the ruling class to frighten the Africans into remaining second class citizens? I had already heard mutterings against the rural education programmes on family planning, as a ploy to keep the blacks under control and the white man in charge.

The only way I felt I could get around this was to ask for the name of the scriptwriter to be changed. I would still write the scripts of course, and bank the cheques, but on air, could they announce the programmes had been written by a black male. Maybe the messages, artfully concealed in the storyline, and coated with humour would have greater impact.

When I traipsed back into the SABC to meet up with Johann, clutching the first three scripts for appraisal, he looked quite shocked when I mentioned this to him.

"Are you sure?" he asked me. "Don't you want your name to be on radio?"

Yes, of course I did, but I was never likely to hear any of the programmes, or understand a word of them. What was I going to do? Listen for the mooing, clucking and bleating sound effects amid the Bantu languages, and think 'I wrote that'?

It took a little while, but eventually Johann could understand where I was coming from and hopefully they did give me another name. However I had to change the length of the programmes, they were all too long. If you have an hour for radio or television, you aim at fifty six minutes, or twenty seven minutes for a half hour programme. This is to leave enough time for the presenter to read the links and any throw-forwards for future programmes. So I had to take them all home again and chop great chunks out.

Now although I had three months in which to write all

thirteen scripts, there was a lot more to it than putting them on paper, laboriously typing them up, delivering them and then waiting for the cheque.

Policy dictated that they had to be evaluated for the target audience, checked for factual errors, and thoroughly discussed by a wide range of people. So a couple of days after delivering the first three, amended scripts, I was summoned back in to Auckland Park and whisked up in the lift to a boardroom on the fifth floor. (That may be incorrect, because to be honest I cannot remember which floor it was on, more literacy licence, but you do remember who is writing this don't you?)

The boardroom had the largest table I had ever seen, binoculars would have been useful when searching for those on the far side of it, but the chairs were quite comfortable. I think I must have been the last to enter. I was not late, but maybe all the other occupants had been given an earlier time, as they all stopped talking and stared at me as I walked in.

There have been many times in my life when I have felt intimidated, and that was certainly one of them. As I took my place, I was introduced to those present, professor this, and professor that, and PhD the other. They were all noteworthy people - well educated, well respected and experts in their field, which I guessed would be education and animal husbandry. There were both black and white Africans, all in business suits, many with greying hair, and all so horribly self assured. And of course, they were all men.

Gingerly I perched on the nearest chair and nodded shyly. I pulled my chair a little closer to the table while trying to make sure that my skirt stayed well over my knees. Just my luck, the nearest chair was slap bang in front of the table leg, forcing me to straddle it either side. If there was one thing my mother taught me, it was that young ladies should always keep their knees together, except I suppose for those rare occasions when we are driven to procreate.

Today was not one of those 'keeping knees together' days. I wriggled a bit on the chair and tried to relax.

All in all the meeting didn't go too badly. In fact they were very complimentary about what I'd written, and it wasn't until I got out to the car that I realized that I, or rather my work, had been the focus of an important board meeting held by the national broadcaster. For a lowly teacher who didn't even have a degree, this was quite a step and my legs shook as I approached my decrepit car among the other shiny, new models in the car park.

I now had *carte blanche* to complete the series, with my basic outlines approved, so all that was left to do was to find the time to write them all.

I continued to get up at five o'clock, and managed an hour before the usual scramble for breakfast, lifts to school for the children and the rush to get me into the classroom several miles further up the freeway.

I usually managed another hour or so in the afternoons, longer if the children disappeared into the garden and were not trying to kill each other, and I would try to sneak off after they had gone to bed to get a few more words down on paper.

When it was all completed and delivered, I breathlessly waited for the cheque.

Since my memory is failing me more and more these days, I'm not sure of the exact chain of events that followed, but I do know we moved house, which thankfully meant no problems with the postal service as we had a mailbox.

I had by now completely saturated the play department, the short story department, the children's programme and Springbok Radio was no more. I had also written about everything I could think of for the magazines, which wasn't difficult because frankly, I was on a different wavelength to the average reader. I had not lived all that long in South Africa, so I was not in a position to give advice about managing maids, or coping with African diseases. Nor could I write about bringing up children or caring for them, I was the reckless woman who had taken a seven week old baby out to live in the bush without inoculations, electricity, transport or money, so what kind of mother was I? I just didn't have a clue what I could write about.

I pondered this problem for a few days and then came up with the answer. Of course, I would write books and take the literary world by storm. Firstly I would resurrect Horatio Tumbletum, bully someone into drawing some illustrations of him, (I can't draw to save my life), and then find an agent.

I put together six of my best stories, constructed a Horatio toy correct in every detail, and ploughed through the South African media directory for an agent. I found one, which was lucky as she was the only one listed, but she lived in Durban, six hundred kilometres away. Nothing daunted I sent her a letter and waited in breathless anticipation. Well not literally you understand, snail mail took several days if it arrived at all, and I would have died of asphyxiation.

To my delight she replied to say that she was travelling to Johannesburg the following week, and she would like to meet me as she was interested in the manuscript I had sent her. Yes! Was I ever ready for the big time! I tried to keep my enthusiasm under control and the family were a great help. They showed not the slightest bit of interest.

I would wrestle magazines out of the tiny post box, ripping them to shreds on the way, and wave them under the noses of my offspring with encouraging words such as "Look, I wrote this, see Mummy's name is here, and this is on sale throughout the whole country! What do you think of that?"

Noncommittal grunts and shrugs of the shoulders were the

only replies I got. My ex was a bit more enthusiastic, but I found it hard to keep a cheerful smile on my face when he announced he'd invited a dozen or so friends over for a *braai* on Saturday. Damn, that meant extra time making salads and whipping round the house to clear up the enormous mess my tribe could scatter in the twenty four hours since the maid had departed on Friday afternoon.

However, I must say they gave me peace and quiet to write most afternoons. As the sun shone in the blue, African sky, they were nearly always out of doors or splashing in the pool. The rule was not to disturb Mummy unless someone was drowning, bleeding to death, had been bitten by a snake or the house was on fire.

There were a few occasions when one of them would run in and scream,

"Mummy! Thomasina (the cat) is playing with a snake in the back yard." OK so it didn't exactly fall into any of the categories above, but it was an acceptable interruption.

I also understood the cry "Mummy, there is a strange man in the garden and he's doing something very funny with his trousers." Yes, that too was enough to bring me instantly back into the real world and send me racing away from my desk and out into the garden, only stopping to grab one of the Bushmen spears off the wall.

But all was not lost. I was going to meet my agent and she would set me on the road to fame and fortune. I waited in breathless anticipation, (yes there was a lot of that in those days, but it sounds better than breathed excitedly don't you agree?) We met at a cafe in a nearby shopping mall and I guessed who she was immediately as a smartly dressed, stately lady approached. We shook hands and sat down, but we did not really connect all that well. You know how it is - you take to some people immediately, feel on the same wave length and... well, *we* didn't.

I gave her the manuscript with all Horatio's stories, the pictures I'd had drawn to show what he looked like, and the stuffed toy. She whipped out a contract and showed me where to sign. It was pages and pages long, and had I taken the time to read it all the way through, we would still have been there the following morning.

It was obvious she was in a hurry, and after drinking a swift cup of coffee she departed, clutching her copy of the contract and the envelope containing Horatio and his world, and that was the last I saw of her.

6 I'M LEAVING SCHOOL

I did hear from her again. She wrote to say she had excellent contacts at Penguin, and Horatio was on his way to England. I sat and crossed my fingers and toes.

The next letter told me that he had been rejected, as 'not being strong enough for the market'. What the hell did that mean? I wrote back to enquire if she was going to try and place my furry creation with other publishers, but she did not reply. I was left to wonder and to this day, I'm still not quite sure what she meant.

I typed up another fantasy book I was writing and sent that off to Durban as well. This time she did reply, saying that she had checked, and as my characters bore the names of Cinderella and Prince Charming, I would be infringing on Walt Disney copyright.

Jumping forward several months, I was passing the television one day, and happened to catch sight of a programme featuring ALF, Alien Life Form. He could almost have been Horatio's twin brother, and guess what, he also had a very loud voice, only he ate cats, not dust and dirt.

A couple of years further down the road, we went to the movies to watch Shrek, and although this time there were lots more differences, they too had used the fairy tale characters as figures of fun. So, there was little hope of me taking the literary world by storm there either. Both manuscripts are still languishing under the bed, and maybe I'll dust them off one day and publish them myself.

Our contract had been for one year, and as the months

flew past, I could not see it being renewed. I was without an agent and I had totally run out of people and places to badger with my written offerings. To add to my woes, the weekly newspaper which was paying me so well, dropped their free edition, so that work dried up too.

I wandered round the house not sure what to do with myself if I wasn't writing. I was still teaching at school of course, but it had been so nice to write knowing that I had been asked to write and also knowing, that I was going to get paid at the end of it. It had been good while it lasted.

The SABC came to the rescue. I was called in by Johann and asked to write another radio series for Informal Black Adult Education. This time the aim was to encourage people to be entrepreneurial. Many people found it difficult to get jobs, especially if they'd not completed their school education. In theory it was compulsory to go to school. In practice, it was not always followed up. Many children dropped out if their parents could not afford the annual fees, which were pennies to us but a fortune for them; or they stopped attending if they could be put to good use herding goats or watching the cattle.

The proposed programmes were aimed at suggesting ways that people could make a living through their own efforts. I thought it was a great idea and waxed enthusiastically about the series in Johann's office, but when I got home, I began to get cold feet.

What on earth was I going to write? I hadn't the faintest idea how one could earn a living from scratch. It wasn't a case of suggesting that they attend night school and make up their education, followed by working their way through university.

Nor doing the kind of work our children in first world countries might choose as part time work after school, such as delivering newspapers, or standing behind the till in the local supermarket. And it was no good punting the 'bob-a-job' approach, because the target audience lived in areas where no one paid people to water their lawns, prune hedges or paint walls. None of those things existed in the informal settlements.

I went into panic mode. I had to think up at least thirteen ideas for making a living with no capital, few facilities, and little education. Many of the listeners would not even be able to read or write.

The children were at a sleep over, my ex was out with the guys from the office and I had the house to myself. I sat down, and had a good long think. I tried to imagine what it was like to live in a shack in a township where I had very little money, surrounded by other people who also had very little money to spend. Again, my mind returned to my days in Botswana, and the people I had met there in the rural areas. It was quite impossible to wander into rural communities in South Africa, and it could be downright dangerous to venture into the townships. This was going to put a serious strain on my imaginative powers.

Suddenly, as so often happened, all the pieces fell into place. I remembered how young Africans love to have their hair done, so one suggestion could be they learn how to plait cornrows and charge a few cents per customer. I thought about planting flowers, or even fruit and vegetables from seed, watering them and then selling the produce, and I explained step by step how to do it. There was also the very informal nursery crèche where small babies and children could be cared for while working mothers were absent. Yes, this was usually done by other family members, but the exodus to the cities was by now quite common, so there may be opportunities in that direction, as families became more fragmented. Again, I explained how to handle that. Of course, there was no worry about registration, or permits or inspections of premises and facilities, these just did not happen in the black areas. I thought about the various handicrafts people could make and then sell, using local products, or even scrap materials or discarded waste. My days teaching art in the infant classes came in handy at this point! Simple toys, made from nothing, which could be sold for a nominal amount. And there was also the idea of buying large bottles of Coca-Cola, a perennial favourite of the Africans, and decanting it into plastic cups and charging enough to allow a small profit plus, the cost of a replacement bottle.

The more I thought about it, the more things I began to think of. How about cleaning cars in the large shopping mall car parks, polishing shoes on the pavement, preparing food to sell by the side of the road, or making snack foods for neighbouring shebeens, the informal African bars selling local homemade beer?

There is a big downfall of fledgling businesses in the third world. Projects will offer funds to set up and stock your outlet, but often once the money comes in, it's all spent, without keeping some back to replace the goods to sell in the following weeks. I made a big fuss about this point in every programme as sustainability was also a vital factor in success.

Generally I was quite impressed with the ideas I had and I think Johann was too. I would love to know if anyone ever followed any of the suggestions that were broadcast. They used actors, of course, to explain what they were doing and how successful they had become. Again, I made sure that each programme told a story and hopefully it entertained at the same time as it taught.

I wrote many more series for Johann, and I really enjoyed doing them. But more was to come.

I was summoned to the SABC again, and this time it was the Pre-School Education Department. Janine was a lovely lady, also Afrikaans, with a great sense of humour. Her mandate was to commission programmes for a daily broadcast for pre-schoolers, up to the age of five, to include songs, stories, games and rhymes. She needed a ten minute daily story, and this time the contract was for fifty two programmes.

I gulped. Could I think up that number of stories? Luckily I didn't have to, not the topics anyway. At yet another meeting at the SABC in one of those gigantic boardrooms, I learned that the main character had already been decided - a crow by the name of Cedric, sponsored by a dried fruit company. I honestly can't remember if Cedric liked raisins and sultanas, but he became a household word in South Africa with his poster on display in every supermarket.

This was followed by a second series featuring a family of chickens who were friends with a horse. Once again, an eminent crowd sat around the table and mapped out the series, listing the various 'lessons' they wanted the young audience to learn.

For both these series there was a tie-up on television, which would use puppets in the daily show, and feature the same character voices which would be used on the radio. The subject matter would be the same for both, but the stories completely different. I was aware that the target audiences for radio and television were likely to be worlds apart.

While most squatter shacks, or in more politically correct speech, 'informal dwellings', (shacks by any other name) possessed a radio, there was a very small percentage which possessed a television set, so the stories on the radio would be less sophisticated and more understandable through the medium of sound.

I had great fun writing this series, even though my wings were clipped a little as I was advised to keep the same characteristics for the different chickens, and I've never had a great affinity for birds. Although I like eggs, especially fried, I prefer my animals furry and cuddly.

Again I beat a path to the SABC, this time to meet a lady called Nancy. She was the commissioning manager for the Formal Education Department Schools Radio Programmes. As you can imagine, the title was in very small letters on her business card.

It must all sound a little confusing, but there were several educational departments within the SABC. Formal and Informal, for blacks and for whites, and then other departments aimed at the adults, high schools, primary schools and pre-school children. It's not important at all if you don't remember them.

Nancy wanted a daily story suitable for little children who were already in school, who could listen with their teachers every morning. Each programme would cover a different topic in the syllabus as laid down by government, and if possible, aim to educate the teachers at the same time by giving them practical ideas on teaching. Educating by chanting was still quite common, imparting knowledge by constant repetition, without stopping to find out if the children had the faintest idea what it was all about. I signed another contract for fifty two programmes.

Since I had so many different series running at the same time - Formal and Informal Pre-School Education, Schools Radio, and Adult Education - I bought reams of paper in different colours and assigned a colour to each series. It was one way of keeping a kind of primitive filing system.

By this time I was running ragged. I had no great illusions about my ability to write. I would never be a Dickens, Agatha Christie or J K Rowling, but it seemed as if I was a reliable hack writer, who always met her deadlines. I have never, ever missed a deadline to this present day. I still get my monthly column in on time and I think by now that Carol the editor, knows if it doesn't appear, it's because the road roller has finally flattened me, or I've been carried off by slave traders.

It occurred to me that I was earning more for writing two programmes, which by now I could scribble in one day, than I earned for a whole month's teaching. Now that I had been writing for a couple of years, I was no longer on the basic writer's rate and the extra Rand for every minute of script, made them quite lucrative. But did I have the courage to give up a solid teaching job with a regular cheque at the end of every month?

I thought long and hard, and acted completely against everything I had been brought up to believe. I handed in my notice.

The staff at school looked at me with pitying eyes. They just knew this was not going to work. I was a teacher, not a writer! They had not seen anything broadcast on television written by me, and to take a chance like this was sheer madness.

I was not sure either, but in a fit of recklessness, I stuck to my decision after a secret meeting with the headmistress, who assured me that if it didn't work out, then I could step back into the next available post.

Now I had the freedom to have more civilized hours, spend more time with the family and even enjoy a bit of a social life as well. I was in my seventh heaven, although there was always that niggly feeling at the back of my mind as to what I was going to do if it all dried up. I'd never seen myself as the self-employed entrepreneurial type.

But maybe I had made it. I was now a fulltime freelance writer, just as I had dreamed of all those years ago. OK, so it wasn't exactly Shakespeare, and writing words for a grumpy horse and an assortment of farmyard chickens was not quite what I had in mind originally, but I was still putting words on paper.

It was also time I moved on from the typewriter to the computer. Too many hours were wasted as I had to retype pages where there was more Typex on the paper than ink, and no sooner had I thought about the idea than my ex returned the following night with a desktop monitor, hard drive box and a keyboard occupying pride of place on the back seat of his car.

If I thought this was going to be an easy transition, I was very much mistaken. Full of enthusiasm, I sat down to write my first script on this new and amazing technology. The title was fine and then I dropped down two lines and began to type. Since I have never been trained to touch type, and even today I watch my fingers and not the text, I didn't notice at first that the words were disappearing off the left of the screen. Where had they gone? I found the delete button and tried again, but the same thing happened, as soon as I typed more than the width of the screen, the text disappeared from view and I couldn't find it anywhere. With deadlines fast approaching I rushed back to the typewriter.

I paid a lady to come in a few days later to show me how it all worked, but she was not a lot of help as the word processing package I had was called Wordstar and she was not familiar with it. However, I managed almost by accident, to set up the page parameters and bit by bit, learn just enough to write scripts and fax headings. Once I had a template for radio scripts and later television scripts, I could cut, paste and copy and then delete the body of the script and start with a fresh, blank outline. I still had to use the typewriter to manually type in the department, programme series and page number on the top of the scripts. I was not yet clever enough to fit all that in on my famous script template.

All went well for quite some time until I allowed a visiting guest to insert one of his floppy disks into the drive so he could play some games. Disaster! It was full of bugs and the next day nothing worked. I panicked and raced into Johannesburg to the computer hospital, explaining my broadcast deadlines and they promised to de-bug it and have it ready in no time at all.

When I went to collect it the following day, they said they had managed to clean up the hard drive, something I didn't even realize my computer had, and they had also managed to reinstall most of the programmes, but nowhere could they find a copy of the ancient Wordstar I'd been using. So now it had a new and improved programme which was much, much better, and I would love it.

No, it wasn't, and no, I didn't.

All the short cuts I had discovered in the old programme now didn't work, and for several weeks I struggled to find the right keys to press. I was in a constant state of panic for days. There is nothing more terrifying than a broadcast deadline, it even obliterates 'writer's block' which just can't be allowed to happen, there just isn't the time.

In the broadcasting world, 'writer's block' is seen as a kind of cop-out, a kind of self-indulgence. Either you can write or you can't, they say and you had better come up with the ideas quickly, or *you* can explain to the viewers why there is nothing on their screens tonight, or just dead air on the radio.

I think this is why many productions are jointly written, or use different writers each week. At a conference I attended in Johannesburg, we were told by one scriptwriter that in America, writers are all herded into a classroom, where they are told the storyline and then instructed to write the dialogue for one, or at most, two of the characters.

I found this very hard to believe at the time, but this young man had moved from Johannesburg to Hollywood and had done very well. He explained the unbreakable formulae all dramas, police series, and serials were based on, how and where the sub plots fitted in, and where, when and how the climax and wrap should be written.

It all sounded so staid, with no wriggle room for creativity, and I was glad I was writing for a less sophisticated broadcasting service which allowed my imagination to soar. He was welcome to his career in Hollywood. It wasn't for me.

I was reminded of one radio programme I wrote telling the story from the point of view of a fly. He was out to make all the people sick, and he was an evil little bastard, but great fun. As soon as it was read by the programme manager I was called in.

"This story is told by a fly, right?"

"Yes. By the name of Basil."

"But how will anyone know that?"

"Uh, well, he tells us in the first line that he's a fly."

"But will the people believe that?"

"Well, I thought they would. In African folklore you have talking animals and talking trees and things, so I thought it would be OK to have a talking fly."

I wasn't getting through, I could sense it. "Look, I can rewrite that episode if you like."

Another important maxim, the Client is always right, even when he's wrong!

"No, no, don't do that just yet. We'll consult on it."

As I left Auckland Park that day, I hoped they would agree as I quite liked Basil, even if he did have evil intentions. I thought they would simply phone me up to say 're-write' or we 'will accept'. But no, I was summoned back in to the Radio Block, into another boardroom and another group of eminent men.

To my amazement, I was introduced as Mrs X who was just coming to observe the meeting. I was not going to take part in the discussion, so it seemed that I would not be allowed to punt for Basil at all.

I sat and listened to the comments as they flew back and forth across the gigantic table and I was rather amused to see that it was only my Afrikaans manager who had any doubts about Basil. Everyone else was very positive indeed, and at the end of the meeting, Basil got his reprieve and a few months later took to the airwaves after all.

Who they thought Mrs X was I have no idea, but surely such eminent people must have guessed that I was the writer. Afterwards I got a lot of positive feedback about Basil, but when I had already been writing for months about talking chickens, a horse and a crow, I'm not sure what all the fuss was about.

7   ON TO TELEVISION

The chickens of Feather Foot Farm, and their horse friend ran its course on the television, and I breathed a sigh of relief at being released from my feathered creatures. I happily imagined them served up for Sunday lunch - only the chickens, not the horse! I was a bit worried that one series had fallen away but I didn't have to worry for long.

For the next series, I had *carte blanche* to choose the scenario, and so Themba and Thuli were born. They lived with their grandmother and grandfather in a rural area, while their mother lived in the city working in one of the big supermarkets. Father worked in the mines and appeared now and again. This was a very common situation in South Africa, where families often live apart and children live with their grandparents, or other family members. They are often passed around like DHL parcels from one family member to another, often in different areas of the country.

It was a lot easier writing about children. I found the dialogue flowed better as I had a greater understanding of the way kids talked, and what they talked about, instead of trying to imagine what topics might be of supreme interest to chickens. For example, as far as I knew, chickens only ever ate bird seed and stuff they pecked off the ground, while children gave me much more scope in the food department alone.

On reflection, I only hoped that I was doing some good,

and that someone, somewhere might follow the good advice which I ladled out in every episode.

Occasionally I stopped to think. What was I doing? It was so presumptuous to imagine I was on the same wavelength of another culture. For example, when I wrote about Themba and Thuli getting a fright when they saw Grandfather pulling his teeth out to wash them after the travelling dental clinic had been; was I putting out the wrong message? Heaven knows I might have been the cause of children having nightmares well into their mid twenties.

I must have created adventures for them for the best part of a year. Later they were picked up by a publisher, but I never got round to writing the books although I meant to. I don't know if anyone else ever put the books together, but I would have no cause to complain if it was a question of copyright.

I've heard people in Britain who work for the BBC complain bitterly about all kinds of things, and although I enjoyed freelancing for the SABC, every time I accepted a contract from them, I signed away any copyright I might like to claim. At first I wasn't even aware of this, and it never occurred to me that I should maintain any intellectual property on my work. The way I saw it was they were paying me to write, and what I produced I handed over in return for the cheque.

I joined SASWA, the South African Scriptwriter's Association, and this opened my eyes. I learned that overseas, scriptwriters were entitled to be paid not only for their initial scripts, but also for rebroadcasts and any further sales to other broadcasters at home or abroad.

The stumbling block was that South Africa was not a signatory to the Berne Convention which set out all these safeguards for writers. We were screwed. If we didn't sign the contract as it stood, then we would not be offered work. It was as simple as that.

At one point we had a great doyen of the theatre as our SASWA President, I could describe her as the Betty Grable equivalent in Hollywood, she had more awards and accolades than we lesser mortals had hot dinners.

In conjunction with a pet lawyer, the top in his field, she went head to head with the SABC and finally got them to agree that all writers signing with them in the future would be eligible for repeat fees if there was more than one re-broadcast. If programmes were sold to other countries, the writer would get an agreed slice of the cake.

The SABC caved in quite easily, so easily we were all more than a little surprised, but not for long. The next time I went in to sign a contract, it looked exactly the same. Identical columns of tiny, tiny writing, exact blue paper, exact places to sign. I couldn't see any difference at all, until I noticed the heading at the top. I wasn't being commissioned by the SABC, I was now engaged by Safritel. This was a new company which did not have to abide by any agreements made with the national broadcaster. Nothing else had changed. We were screwed again, and life went on as before. No wonder they had agreed so quickly, they had already come up with plan B and there was nothing we could do about it.

Yes, we all grumbled and moaned and groaned, but the top class pet lawyer had moved on and we all still needed to earn a living.

SASWA was more successful with dealing with a small group of wannabe scriptwriters who were punting their services well below industry rates. It wouldn't work with the SABC as they had fixed rates for new, midterm and established writers, but it might be tempting for the smaller production companies. Most of these belonged to the National Television and Video Association. Any professional association membership gave you credibility, so it was agreed by everyone, that rates were fixed between certain parameters to protect everyone, and this time it worked.

One SABC series followed the next, and altogether I must have written a couple of thousand scripts for radio. At the peak of my writing I had three programmes on daily, five days a week, each either ten or fifteen minutes long, and the money rolled in. Unfortunately it rolled out again, as my ex, bless him, was never a reliable provider, and he changed jobs with monotonous regularity.

I was constantly living in overdraft, but I consoled myself that I was owed a lot of money which would eventually arrive once the wheels of the finance department of the SABC ground round. I was a little alarmed when they decided to stop paying out every fortnight and changed that to once a month.

On the last Friday of the month I would stand in the queue with lots of well known TV stars and other personalities as we waited to collect our money. If there had been any screw up in the accounts department and the cheque wasn't there, you knew you had to wait another thirty plus days, and this was a worry.

I had two short lean spells in the following five years, when my managers informed me they had been told they were to share the work around a little more. They wanted to commission me, but had been instructed to use new writers, which I guess was fair.

On the first occasion I rushed off to sell houses, at which I was absolutely hopeless. The buyers didn't know what they wanted, and the sellers knew what they wanted but would never get, even if their property was on the market for a millennium.

I would make appointments for viewing, collect the clients and then drive them around.

"Oh, we saw this one this morning, and we didn't like it,"

they would exclaim.

I'd smile as I left them in the car and went to apologize to the hopeful house seller, muttering under my breath. I had told them exactly where I was taking them, complete with pictures of the property. Surely they could have mentioned they had already viewed the place?

I tried hard to keep my patience as people who firmly stated they would only buy a four bedroomed house, cheerfully bought a three bedroomed one from another agent. I reined in my temper when couples told me their house was worth more than all the others in the same street, when everyone could see *their* house was the only one falling down.

On the second occasion I raced off to sell insurance, but the cold calling and getting referrals was terrifying, and signing people up to policies you guessed they couldn't afford, and which would not meet their needs, just wasn't for me. The day I watched a young couple scribble their signatures on the contract for health cover in pregnancy, when I knew it only covered them from the third day after the birth, I walked out. I'm sure there are lots of responsible insurance salesmen out there, so maybe I had picked a bad company, but it was not for me.

In desperation I took to marketing myself, which wasn't easy as I am basically shy. I typed up the most interesting resume I could, obtained a copy of the directory listing all the production houses in South Africa, and phoned every one of them, but not before I'd had a couple of glasses of wine, lit a cigarette and taken several deep breaths.

"I am the best writer on the planet since Charles Dickens," I told them and if they would only let me write one script for free, or spare a few moments for a meeting, I would prove how good I was.

When I think of it now I cringe, but the bills had to be paid and I was quite determined that I was not going to sell insurance or houses and I was not going back into the classroom. I certainly wasn't any good at the first two and the way things were going, we would starve in record time.

I was saved one morning when I got a telephone call asking me if I was interested in writing for television. Do ducks like water? This was it, this was the breakthrough at last.

I was ready for the big time!

I was extremely nervous and excited when I went along to the production house to find out what they wanted. It was a series on SABC called 'Impact', along the lines of 'Tomorrow's World', and I think there was a similar series in Australia, showing all the new gadgets and technologies coming onto the market, or in the final stages of research and development.

For many companies, it was a low cost way of getting five or ten minutes of television advertising, and they were also given the programme afterwards to use for their in-house training or trade fair promotions. It was a good deal for them, and a good deal for the 'Impact' team, although the budgets were not enormous and that is what nearly ended my TV career right then and there.

I drove out to the very smart production offices north of Pretoria to meet the staff and the first person I met was a brilliant manager called Bob, who helped me through. He was a fund of information and only too happy to help. I don't know where he had heard about me, but he needed another writer on the team, so here I was sitting on the other side of his desk one Monday morning.

Now, up until this point I had been able to write pretty much what I wanted within a certain theme. I could fly my characters up to the moon, or take them to London, Paris or

New York. I could change the weather, add all the sound effects I wanted and travel backwards and forwards in time. Television is not like that.

To begin with you have a budget, and you need to know the cost of actors, camera hire, tapes, a sound recordist, lighting, location and transport costs and where you can and cannot film. Those are just the basics.

Bob was amazing, and he explained so much to me before I left his office for two further interviews with the top guy Professor Something, and the subject specialist, Professor Something Else.

I went home reeling under all the new restraints that were now going to completely stuff up my creativity. I felt there was no room to manoeuvre, no great soaring scenarios like 'Gone with the Wind'. This wasn't Hollywood, with an MGM budget, this was daytime television produced under corporate sponsorship. Now I had to put my feet firmly on the ground and write about real life as cheaply as possible, while being outstandingly entertaining.

I walked away with instructions to write about sisalation for a national aluminium company. No, I didn't know what it was either, but I was armed with dozens of pamphlets and brochures which I was assured explained it all quite clearly. It didn't. Not to me anyway.

I struggled to understand the difference between convection, diffusion, conduction, advection and radiation. Add to that more information on kinetic energy, transfer of heat, and the change in internal energy. This was not going to be much fun to write at all.

As I struggled to make sense of it, I carefully tabulated the columns I would need to write the video in the left hand column and the audio on the right, with a space in the middle to indicate the length of time each shot should be. I spent a very long time making up this template, which I kept for years, copying it and then deleting the contents of the previous script for each new one. Actually, I spent an inordinate amount of time on it. I was procrastinating big time.

Finally I went the saucepan route, comparing how water heats up in an aluminium pan and in a steel pan. This then led on to the actual sisalation itself which is an insulation material you put inside your roof to keep the heat in and the cold out, or vice versa.

I had become used to arriving in Auckland Park, whizzing up in the lift with my latest batch of scripts, popping in to have a quick chat and a cup of revolting SABC coffee, (not to be recommended), or a more leisurely lunch with my commissioning managers in the staff canteen, where the coffee was marginally better, and then off I would go again.

Now things were very different. My 'Impact' scripts were checked by two experts who liberally covered them in bright red and green corrections, one colour for each. If I could read anything at all by the time I got them back it was a miracle, especially that first one.

However, as time went on, I improved a little, and I became an incredible bore at any social gathering. I had covered so many different subjects and I learned a very little about each one, usually forgotten quite promptly as I moved on to the next topic.

I must add a really important piece of information here. When big Hollywood moguls make movies, they are said to 'film' because of course they use 35mm film in their humongous cameras. I'm not sure if they still do. When you are on a more lowly level, like our video teams, producing for television and corporate events and conferences and so on, we say we are shooting. So forget about the guns, we mere mortals shoot with a camera.

I was a little alarmed when they called me into the

production office and informed me that MEDUNSA, the Medical University of South Africa, which was set up specifically for black Africans, wanted some 'Impact' programmes.

Now, the official blurb is that MEDUNSA was established in 1976 to provide tertiary education and training facilities to the educationally disadvantaged in the fields of Medicine, Allied Health and Nursing Sciences and Dentistry, intended to meet the needs of the country.

They had paid for three inserts, so would I drive up there and find three interesting topics? This was a daunting task, and once again my acting skills came to the fore as I pretended that I thought it well within my capabilities.

The university had been built thirty five kilometres north of Pretoria, and I felt a little nervous as I turned off the main road and into the rural areas close by the large township called Ga-Rankuwa. Even to this day, I find it amazing that the magic of television should result in very eminent and important people welcoming ignorant little me, showing great deference and hospitality as again I was ushered into an imposing boardroom. Internally I shrivelled up. What if they found out I didn't even have a degree?

After much discussion, it was agreed that I would write one script for the Dental Department on mouth guards, another would feature the use of their nuclear medicine and a third department also wanted to show off their hand and micro surgery techniques. I scribbled frantically, trying to forget that I fainted at the sight of blood. It really hadn't occurred to me that I would be required to actually look at anything gory. I was in for a nasty surprise.

When I was swept into a bright, white laboratory, the first thing I saw was a microscope on a table.

"Look down the lens," the professor instructed.

Tentatively, I bent forward. It was quite disgusting - lots of bits of flesh and tiny nerves and other indescribable body parts. I blinked and moved away quickly. It was then I noticed that lying on the plate below the lens was a mouse, breathing slowly because it was out for the count, and what I had just witnessed close up, was the repair to a paw that had been cut off and then partly sewn back on again.

"We are now ready to reattach human hands and feet," they told me bursting with pride.

"Great, uh, brilliant," I replied with my breakfast threatening to burst into the outside world.

It got worse. They showered me with pamphlets, photos and case notes to explain the whole procedure in nauseating detail, while I tried hard to focus on my notebook and the tiled floor. That was possibly the fastest script I ever wrote, and I never once watched the finished programme.

The Dental Department wasn't much better. They were very keen to show me horrific pictures of the damage young men could sustain by not wearing mouth guards while playing contact sports. At least this time, I could write in scenes showing schoolboy rugby and long shots of patients in dental chairs, which was OK as long as I didn't have to get too close. I also got a Springbok rugby player on the programme to say a few words on how important it was to wear protection, and he removed his own mouth guard to show us all. It was a bit gross though.

The Nuclear Department was amazing, and after handing me some special gloves, they let me hold a really heavy jar which contained radioactive material. I'm ashamed to say that I can't remember much about the content of these programmes now, but everyone was happy with the results, and the university ordered two more five minute programmes.

So it was back to the Dental Department to see how they cast false teeth in a special ceramic material which was a break though in using new methods, and then a visit to the

Veterinary Department.

Now this is going to be good, I thought to myself, as I love animals. But no, guess what, they were performing laser surgery on all kinds of animals and while not as gory, it was quite gory enough for me. They positioned this cow next to a large steel plate and tied it up. I thought this was a very strange thing to do until I saw them tilt the table into a horizontal position, and hey presto, there was the cow lying flat on the operating table. After sedating the animal they then blasted away at it with long lasers, and by the time the smell of burning flesh hit me, I was retching on the other side of the paddock.

There were two interesting offshoots from my visit north to the university, and the first one was to provide a real learning experience for me - another of life's lessons.

I was hanging around the Veterinary Department waiting for the relevant professor when I happened to notice a group of people from the nearby township who had brought their pets to the free clinic. I got chatting to them and was a bit puzzled when they told me that the Doctor put lots and lots of needles into their animals to make them well. I assumed they meant the odd injection or inoculation, but no, they told me lots, you know, lots of needles, lots of them, all over, in the paws and the neck and the back and the tummy.

I didn't really believe them and mentioned the strange conversation to the vet when he appeared.

"That's quite correct," he told me. "I practice acupuncture on the animals and it has been very successful."

Acupuncture on animals! I thought this quite brilliant and on the weekend, I went to visit one of his satisfied customers who ran a stud farm north of Johannesburg. Yes, they told me, the vet came and stuck lots of needles in one of their horses and it recovered in no time at all.

I then travelled south of Johannesburg and met a lady whose dog had had numerous behavioural problems and after being punctured all over, without uttering a squeak, it too had recovered quickly and permanently. I was so impressed - I still am - as this would prove that an ancient healing art must work, animals couldn't, and wouldn't, pretend.

Full of enthusiasm, I drove into Auckland Park and went to talk to the producer of the best wildlife series on the SABC. He was equally enthusiastic and thought it would make a great insert. I could go ahead and script it for him, but I also had to find a couple of eminent people to interview who had the opposing viewpoint, and tell us that acupuncture does *not* work.

I was incensed. "But it does work! If animals recover, it must be true!"

"We must present a balanced programme. We have to show both sides of the story," the producer explained. "That allows the audience to make up their own minds."

Great. As far as I was concerned, I wanted to make up their minds for them. I was going to tell them the truth. As far as I was concerned, the recovery of several animals was absolute and infallible proof, and I wanted to tell it to the world, or South Africa at least, and I had no intentions of allowing other people to poke holes in my argument.

I never did make that programme, but it was a lesson I should have learned at the time. Later, watching other programmes on television, I would get angry at one sided documentaries, but that is exactly what I had been trying to do. That producer was right, my programme would not have been balanced.

It was while I was chatting to one of the professors, as we walked through the extensive manicured grounds of the university on the way to the Veterinary Department, that I came to hear of another groundbreaking invention that began right here. Since I had already scripted the five programmes they had paid for, I would have to find a sponsor if I was going to feature this amazing breakthrough. I found out that much of the research had been funded by one of the major banks, so I made an appointment and beat a path to their head office in the middle of Johannesburg.

They were polite and charming, and after I explained about the benefits of featuring their protégé on television on three of the four channels, and also providing them with a social responsibility video for them to use at conferences, trade fairs and so on, they became very enthusiastic. The letter we received at the office confirmed their intention to fund an insert twice the length we usually made. I was ecstatic, but there was a catch. The professor who had invented this groundbreaking technology had never allowed any publicity before, and it was doubtful that he would now. Taking a deep breath, I dialled his number and he invited me to tea at his Pretoria residence.

As I drove up to his palatial home, I looked around to see if there was anywhere I could hide my ancient banger, extra loud now as there was a small hole in the exhaust. But the man was charm itself. Summing up in moments I was a total wuss when it came to biology type stuff, he played his 'get out of jail card'.

He would allow me to make a programme about his work if I watched him operate. It was my worst nightmare. I still went weak at the knees every time I walked into a hospital and fainted at the sight of a saline drip. Now he wanted me IN the operating room to watch! I froze to my chair, in danger of crushing the bone china teacup I was holding. But having got this far, there was no going back. (We could imagine a bit more aspen quivering here, it's just the right place for it, and add it in again a few lines down for yourself if you like).

91

I agreed.

As I entered Ga-Rankuwa Hospital a few days later, I could not quite believe what I had let myself in for. By the time I had on the green scrubs, complete with hat and mask and fetching green bootees to colour co-ordinate, I was ready to pass out.

Looking firmly at the floor, I shuffled behind the friendly nurse and followed her into the theatre. They waved me to a small, round, revolving stool where I could perch out of harm's way. I can cope I told myself, that is until they urged me to look up at the TV screen where I would be able to see quite clearly what was going on. As if I wanted to! While I could possibly pretend to look, I could not avoid hearing the running commentary.

"Now I am about to slice down on the edge of the cornea here, and expose the..." I swayed on my stool and the anaesthetist began to look alarmed. He had two patients to monitor, the lady who was out for the count and me, who was about to meet the floor.

"Are you OK?" he kept asking me as I swayed like a willow tree on my small perch, and this is where we add the extra couple of aspen leaves.

"Fine," I quaked as the floor danced in interesting waves backwards and forwards. It was perhaps a blessing that I could not see the expression on the surgeon's face as he worked away, explaining exactly what he was doing for my benefit, only I wished he wouldn't!

It seemed to take several years for him to remove the cataracts from both eyes, insert the new plastic lenses and then laser the bits of the eyeball safely back into place.

As I slithered to my knees while they wheeled the patient out, I swore never, ever again would I set foot inside another operating theatre. Little did I know that it was going to be the first of many visits in the future.

The rest of the programme was fine; I happily took notes as patients had their eyes tested - I could cope with that. I had immense regard for the professor who had invented and developed the equipment for cataract and laser eye surgery, creating the tiny metal knives and pincer things that enabled it to become an everyday operation which has saved the sight of millions of people, including me.

8   CARPET TILES AND SPY FISH

I came across another amazing project in a building tucked away in the extensive grounds of the university. I guess you could call it a small hostel, where they housed very young girls who had become pregnant and been thrown out by their families. Many of them had no idea they were expecting babies - often it was the result of rape. When they were found, they were brought into the centre and given a comfortable bed and fed, and after their little ones were born, they were taught how to look after them.

The professor in charge of the unit was a warm, caring man and he lent me many books on health. In return, I wrote a small booklet for him, which was published by Heinemann. I refused to take any money for this, as they were struggling for funds as it was. We eventually made a programme on the project sponsored by the Consolidated Goldfields Trust.

With the magic of television beckoning, I learned so much, most of which I promptly forgot. We filmed, or rather shot, in all kinds of places. At one location I was informed that you should never keep products on the shelves for too long, as even the most robust items have a finite shelf life. I got to peer into vast vats of chemicals before they were pressed into tablets and was told that vitamins are a useless waste of money unless they are pre-digested. Fascinating, but have you ever read that on the side of the box? How can you tell?

One of their programmes showed how a certain combination of vitamins made your child brighter at school. It was promptly withdrawn as infringing the advertising standards protocol.

In a factory where they made telephones, I stared in horror at all the employees who were tied to their benches. Before I could accuse them of slave labour, they hurriedly explained this was purely to keep them grounded, in the static electricity sense.

It was around this time that the SABC began to get a bit sticky. The contract for the 'Impact' programmes stated there was only to be a certain amount of advertising in each insert, which was really minimal. But the salespeople who had been visiting companies to get them to sign up for the series had been promising rather a lot more product exposure than was strictly allowed. In fact I think they promised them the earth - almost unlimited advertising all the way through.

The camera crews were quite happy to oblige and so both the voice overs and the interviews freely mentioned the companies and their products.

However the quality control department in Auckland Park, (referred to by us as Awkward Park), began to complain loud and long, and we were told to cut out all this free advertising. If sponsors wanted more exposure, then they would have to pay megabucks for a proper advertisement, and flight it at the exorbitant prices charged by the national broadcaster. To flight a programme or an advertisement means simply to broadcast it, a little more in-house jargon here.

We found a way round it, of course. If we interviewed anyone, we placed them right in front of a board sporting their company logo. We ensured that any employees featured wore clothing with the branding prominently displayed, and of course all the close ups showed the product stamped with the name of the manufacturer. We became experts in focusing the shots to give each sponsored insert as much 'free' advertising as we could.

The guys at the SABC were not stupid; they realized what we were doing, and of course they questioned it. However, we had lots of reasons and excuses why we had pushed the boundaries, such as:

"Under the sign board was the only available place for that interview, away from noise from the factory or the traffic outside."

"All employees are required by law to wear those overalls, and it is not our fault if the company sees fit to print very large logos on their clothing."

Since the SABC were not going to leave their air conditioned offices to check out the various locations, we were quite safe.

Sometimes we shot in the studio, and I remember one particular programme where this was necessary because the client was not going to allow us to get within a million miles of their factory or processing plant. They made a wide variety of household cleaners and beauty products, and boxes of these were delivered to the studio. We were all very intrigued - each one of us was eying up what we intended to take home after the shoot, as we'd heard the products worked well, but were incredibly expensive.

The props lady had bought in several carpet tiles and some indelible felt tip markers. We were going to deface the brand new tile and then clean it off with the chemicals, using a well known presenter. We could afford her for this programme as we saved on travel expenses and time getting to an outside location.

There were plenty of clean backup tiles, and there was much discussion on ways of holding the carpet tile in front of the camera so that in edit, the shots could be spliced together from a dirty to a clean one. The cameraman was also reminded that he must take a lot of cutaways. (These are the extra shots you use when you want to move from one place to another, like a bridging shot. They are also very useful when you are interviewing someone with their face on camera. People move when they speak, so if you are cutting out part of a sentence, or only choosing certain sentences in the programme, you use a cutaway. You may have seen this on television when an interviewee is talking to the camera and the speech doesn't flow and the head jerks around like a puppet on a string. They forgot to shoot cutaways).

We were running a little against the clock on this one. Some idiot had negotiated an hourly rate for our famous personality instead of a fixed price for the job, so no one was going to waste any time. The carpet tile was duly defaced by a crew member's small daughter who had been dragged in for the occasion. Poor little scrap, she couldn't believe she was being asked to scribble over a brand new carpet tile. She was also in awe of the famous personality, who was hung over, in a particularly bad mood, and patently did not want this job, she saw it as a professional form of prostitution. In those days it was not cool to appear in advertisements - it indicated you were desperate for work!

Everything was going well until the cleaning product was used and the marks miraculously disappeared with little or no effort at all.

"F**king hell, would you look at that!" exclaimed the presenter. "It f**king works!"

"Perfect take," called out the director, "except for the language dear. Let's try that again. Take two."

"Bloody amazing!" cried the personality, "I must get some of this s**ding stuff!"

"That's toned it down a little," said the director in exasperation, "but no swear words right? Just use the words we asked you to learn, and it appears that you haven't. Try to keep to the script please, there's a good girl."

In the meantime the sound man had his hands over his daughter's ears and was trying to manhandle her out of the studio. She was resisting him quite successfully, open mouthed at the naughty words she was hearing from one of her idols.

It was just as well props had bought in a good supply of carpet tiles as it took several takes to finally get it right.

Much to our dismay, as soon as the shoot was over, a company representative rushed onto the floor and packed away every last bottle, packet, sachet and sample and triumphantly bore them off back into the waiting van. We didn't even get a look in. I personally boycotted their products after that. How mean can you get? Most jobs have the odd perk, but we were not getting ours that day.

'Impact' made a programme for a toothpaste company, so I got to see inside the laboratories at Wits University in Johannesburg, and yet another school where they were using puppet props to teach the children the foods that were best for their teeth. I begged the company to let us see how they actually made the toothpaste. I was dying to know how they got those red and blue stripes down the centre, and how they squeezed all that white stuff into those little metal tubes. But they refused, the factory was off limits. I was so disappointed. It would appear it was some sort of state secret, and it makes you wonder what they put in it. In later years, I got into many different processing plants, but never into one that made toothpaste.

However, I did learn, from the experts, that you only need a length of toothpaste on your brush the size of your smallest fingernail. I've never forgotten that, and I'm sure it has saved me hundreds of Euros over the years. So you can forget all those advertisements you see on television which show the toothpaste from one end of the brush to the other. Not necessary, they just want you to use it up faster and buy more.

Now, if you follow that advice, think of how much money I've saved you, so it was worth buying this book, wasn't it?

I had visited several factories producing food, but it was when I made a couple of programmes about a large bakery chain that I learned another lesson.

There were a couple of interviews with one of the managers when I carefully wrote down all the information they wanted included in the programme - how many vehicles there were, the number of loaves baked per day and so on. I scurried off home and wrote the script, and returned to their offices a few days later, feeling that they would probably be quite pleased with my efforts.

They weren't.

We were all sitting in an imposing boardroom, a range of directors and managers and I. As I gazed at the impressive art collection, the shimmering reflections leaping off the huge table and the photos of past presidents adorning the walls, these eminent men read it through in front of me. I began to get an uneasy feeling in the pit of my stomach as they all began to shake their heads. One by one, they took pens out of their top pockets and began to strike out scene after scene after scene.

Now, had it been a programme on a subject such as atomic fusion or even that sisalation one I mentioned earlier, I could understand it. But how could anyone go wrong writing down the facts about a bakery? I was about to find out.

"Wrong number of trucks," remarked one guy.

"I agree, and we don't bake as many loaves as that either."

"And too many ovens as well," added a third important man.

I was astounded. I sneaked a look at my notes, surely I could not have got those facts and figures *so* wrong? The numbers I had written down in the interview tallied with those in the script. Had I been daydreaming?

"Come back next week with the correct figures," I was instructed and I tried to crawl invisibly out of the room, which incidentally, is not an easy thing to do.

The following week I was only confronted by one of the managers, who again trawled through the revised script.

"Tsk, tsk, no, it's 159 trucks," he muttered, "only 40,000 donuts a day, and we don't make fairy cakes anymore."

"Can we synchronize these figures?" I asked tentatively. We did.

The following day I was back in and this time I was shown into a different office occupied by a different manager. He pointed to an uncomfortable looking chair on the other side of his desk and perused the script.

"No, too many trucks," he murmured, scoring his pen through the relevant paragraph. "And where are the fairy cakes? They're one of our best sellers. Why haven't you included them? Didn't you see them on the production line when you were shown around the factory?"

"Well, yes, but..." I was lost for words. I knew nothing about the world of big business and the boardroom directors and the various managers of different divisions and their day to day interactions.

"Can you please tell me the exact number of trucks, and how many fairy cakes, and can I make a list of all the products you want included?"

"You will have to check with the transport division on the trucks, but these are the lines I want you to mention...."

So, he *wasn't* sure about the number of trucks, so why did he say I'd got it wrong? I escaped back to the office and wailed to the producer. What was the matter with me? I couldn't even take a simple list of products and vehicles and ovens and workers, without getting them all wrong! I just knew

100

I had the early onset of dementia.

Bob laughed at me. "And what did it say on the tape?" he asked.

"What tape?" I replied.

"On your tape recorder," he said.

"I don't have a tape recorder."

"Then go get one."

In all the to-ing and fro-ing, it had not entered my head that these top executives could be wrong and I could be right! I dug into my meagre savings, walked into the next meeting and plonked my new tape recorder firmly on the boardroom table in full sight. They did a double take and their faces were a picture. One by one they left the room, returning with piles of paper, files and spreadsheets. Finally, I was given the correct figures, which was a big relief as I had forgotten to buy batteries for the tape recorder.

This was an amazing glimpse into the world of the corporate executive, opening the door to a world which did not run as smoothly or as cohesively as the outsider is led to believe. By the time I had completed the approved script, I was beginning to think that I knew more about their company than they did.

It was rare that any script would be accepted on the first reading. The quality control department in the production house was the first port of call, and then they let the client loose on it only after they were satisfied it met their aims and objectives.

Now I know I shouldn't say this, but to me all this jargon is pretty unnecessary. I know there is a difference between an aim and an objective, but do we really have to be so finicky? You simply need to know what information your client wants in the programme and who is going to watch it, it's as simple as that.

We knew who we were supposed to be aiming at with the

101

'Impact' programmes and it was pretty impossible. Inserts were to be entertaining, fast moving to engage the attention of a child, with facts thrown in to interest those at postgraduate level. Frankly you can't be all things to all people, and you may be surprised to know that the average programme on American television is aimed at fourteen to seventeen year olds.

And while I'm at it, another little bit of insider information you might not have come across. In South Africa we tended to follow the American television format and change the visual every three seconds. In British TV, the tendency is to keep a visual on screen for four seconds or longer, not necessarily in dramas, but for news inserts and documentaries, this is the general guideline.

I asked why there was a difference, and was told the British have a longer attention span than the Americans, but I suspect it had more to do with the pace of life. Even today I find some British television programmes drag and move very slowly, but in South Africa, we were used to watching a lot of imported programmes from the United States, and we used these as a benchmark.

But back to those difficult customers. One of my worst clients was high up in the Aluminium Federation, and my heart sank the moment I sat down on the other side of his desk.

"I've always wanted to be a writer," he told me with a smile.

I hate those words. If you really want to be a writer, then you write, it's as simple as that, good, bad or indifferent. Writers are driven to write. They just can't help themselves, it's like a disease you have from birth. People who *talk* about it seldom, if ever, *do* it.

It took quite a while to get the facts out of him as he kept bombarding me with questions about working in the media, and how he could get involved. He hated his job in the corporate world. Eventually, after about an hour, I managed to pin him down and find out what was to go into the programme, and what was to be left out.

I was quite pleased with my first script for him, as there are lots of interesting facts about aluminium and I felt quite confident as I handed over the initial draft. It was returned covered in red pen marks. Never mind, I would put in all the corrections as required. Draft two came back equally plastered with remarks, this time in green pen. I laboured away, swapping scenes around, reconnecting the audio, inserting new visuals and presented it again. The remarks this time were in a sort of purplely violet hue. I decided that the cost of petrol driving in and out of the city would soon swamp any money I might make and so I faxed my next re-write, and the next, and the next, and the next.

In all, I did thirty two variations on a theme until finally, the client was satisfied. As a matter of curiosity, I compared version thirty two with version one and they were almost identical. Another learning curve - I now explained firmly to clients that I was happy to do up to five re-writes in the price of the script, but more than that and there would be extra charges. This brave pronouncement also partly solved my problems with incorrect information. I had learned that money talks.

Working on the 'Impact' programme was great fun, partly because it was so varied, and partly because I am so nosey. In a quiet moment, having seen how the Production Secretary was running ragged, I listed the necessary props and a location list below the script. She was ecstatic and begged me to do that for all my scripts, and a few written by other people as well. This led to more involvement on the practical side and before I knew it, I was acting as the Production Secretary's Assistant as well. This was even more fun, and it was gratifying to be involved, and see the script come to life, and experience so many different places and varying kinds of work.

Then came the day when it all became too much for the PS and she stormed out, and guess who was around at the time when there was a deadline for a broadcast, and who was now writing scripts and helping with all the pre-production work as well? Not that I was complaining they paid me by the day and the money was good.

Then there seemed to be further shortages of staff. Someone rushed off to get married, another one had a nervous breakdown, and next thing I knew, I was climbing into the production van and setting off as a sort of gofer on shoot. This was just magic. I'd written dozens of scripts and I had seen the finished programmes, but never the in-between bits. Now I was out there on the ground and I loved it.

I would liaise with the boss' secretary first thing in the morning, noticing with amusement how she ripped the final approved script out of its smart, plastic folder, tearing the pages apart so she could make several photocopies, while I grabbed one and worked out what was required.

I needed to work out the right order to shoot the scenes, where we were going to shoot, plan the route to take, book the actors, get permission to film, reserve the vehicles and list the props and, if necessary, the costumes. But only after I called the met office to check on the weather, as most of our work was out of doors.

I was particularly delighted the day I called the posh school in Pretoria, (yes the one that had given me the boot), to ask permission to use their balcony for a Romeo and Juliet scene, but I can't for the life of me remember what the topic was now. I do remember that Romeo ripped his tights getting out of the van and the cameraman had to shoot round that. I think he could only show him from the waist up. Such a shame, they were nice green tights hired from the local theatre. I decided I would get someone else to take them back.

Without mentioning any names, I also wrote a programme for a photographic company, which processed thousands of films in the days before the one-stop shop with its in-house processing machine was common on the High Street. It was, in all but name, the exact same outfit as the one belonging to an American company which had pulled out due to sanctions against the apartheid government. Amazingly it had the same staff, the same buildings and machinery, the same infrastructure, the same everything. The only things that had changed were the logo and the company name. I wondered how many other companies had disinvested on paper only. The interesting titbit I picked up on this shoot was that after processing and printing films, they collected quite a large residue of silver. I'd not known that before.

There is a government offshoot in South Africa with three branches, which is essentially an enormous think tank and research facility and I was let loose in their Pretoria campus. I was thrilled, I was able to be as nosey as I liked. It stretched over a wide area, dozens of small and medium buildings housing researchers in all different branches of science and engineering.

We made a programme about a certain fish which was bred to live in a large glass tank secured to the river bank, downstream from dubious factories, to monitor any waste products which may find their way into the water. The 'spy fish', as I thought of it, would give the game away immediately by either getting sick, or going to the big fishpond in the sky if any pollutants were poured into the water.

I learned that the programme was destined for the International Water Convention being held that year in

Brighton, England and I would love to know what the reaction was. I imagine in the first world they had lots of scientific measuring instruments, all high tech stuff, while here in Africa, a group of small fish seemed to work just as well. But maybe the 'Society for the Protection of the Mental State of Fish', or some other tree hugging society would soon put a stop to that.

We also filmed the establishment's educational initiatives to raise awareness of the importance of drinking clean water. I watched in horror as two young children came to collect water in a small village dam, right next to a urinating cow. They struggled off with the bucket carried between them containing more urine than rancid, stagnant water. I promise you, those people are tough.

Often we would go out into the rural areas to film. Usually on arrival we would have to get permission from the local chief before we started rolling the camera, and we often had to sit and wait a long time.

We covered a new tank installation near a town called Hammanskraal, funded by foreign aid. Tall steel cylinders towered above us, full of fresh, clean water, a boon for the women who no longer had to spend hours fetching it in buckets from the river. Now they could wash clothes and dishes next to their houses. The village chosen for this prototype was, like most African villages, next to the road and not near the river. The men who designed this wanted easy access to transport, and were not in the slightest bit worried that it took hours to reach the nearest source of water.

We needed help from the local inhabitants to show how they used the water, and everything was going well until one man appeared who strongly objected.

"These women are not cheap labour!" he screamed. "I know people get lots of money for being on the television, what are you going to pay me?" We weren't featuring him at all, but this seemed to have escaped his notice entirely.

The cameraman tried to reason with him, explaining that the people who were paid were professional actors, who had to learn lines and so on and so on, but our angry man was having none of it. He knew that stars in the movies and in television earned megabucks, and he wanted his share. There was no reasoning with him.

I was at a loss as to how to convince him we didn't have that sort of money. As usual there was not a spare penny in the budget to pay any cast, and we were only filming the women going about their everyday lives. But life is a learning curve, and this was the first time I tried a trick that I later used again and again out on location.

I steered the angry man a little way away from the camera and took his whole attention, listening intently to what he had to say and distracting him from the cameraman who simply continued rolling the camera in the background.

We managed to escape, as we had got the shots we needed, but back at the studio we had a brainstorming session.

"We can hardly hide in the bushes and shoot, now can we?"

"But we need to show people using the stuff, or whatever it is."

"Buckets."

"What?"

"Buckets. And bowls. Plastic ones in bright colours. That's how we'll pay these impromptu actors."

It was a brilliant idea and it worked so well. Now, every time we packed the crew van, we also added piles of washing up bowls, buckets and a linen basket or two. It must have looked strange to any passerby, and I'm sure a Hollywood crew would turn their noses up in disgust, but it did the trick and we always got complete cooperation from anyone we asked to role-play for us. Only after we were happy with the footage were they presented with a shiny new bucket or bowl in return.

Sadly, a couple of weeks later, we were told to pull the plug on the water tank programme, as those indestructible-looking steel cylinders had been vandalized. Not only were they damaged once, it happened again and again and again, every time the engineers came out to repair them.

It took a lot of research until they finally found out the truth. The young men in the village strongly objected to the easy access to water. Previously, they had followed the young girls to the river while they fetched water or washed clothes. It was a time to flirt, and tease them and possibly choose a future wife. If the housework was done close to home, there was no opportunity for courting, so the obvious answer was to destroy the water tanks and force the young women to return to the river.

Someone, somewhere had not done their homework and taken the social customs into consideration. It was back to the drawing board.

9   TOPICS AT RANDOM

Each day brought a different topic, a different venue and a different story to tell.

One really revolting place where I went on a recce was a leather factory. The workshop where they dyed and made the sofas and chairs was fine and I was fascinated to see that they stapled everything together. It was the processing plant that had me threatening to throw up. The skins were brought in from all over the area, often in ones or twos by local herdsmen. These all went into large revolving drums where they were mixed with some liquid which removed all the fat. I can promise you that the smell was indescribable. Out of consideration for the camera crew, and just in case I was listed on the crew to shoot this one, I severely limited the number of scenes showing the initial process.

I also got to see inside the company which printed monthly statements of accounts for different companies. If you never gave much thought to the paper bills we all received every month before the computer took over, you may also have been astounded at the automation required to send these out in their hundreds of thousands. Computers the size of Portakabins, on a specially sprung floor, and kept at optimum temperature hummed away, while reams and reams of paper spewed out over rollers as they were printed and addressed.

I had, and still have, a fascination for assembly lines and the amazing machines that sort, package, fill, separate and seal the vast variety of products for the consumer market. I could stand and stare at them for hours.

The largest assembly plant I visited made Nissan cars, it was enormous. It was also a bit scary as people kept using those bright welding torches, and while it might be very uncomfortable to be standing next to a worker who suddenly turned on a welding torch right next to you, when he was wearing goggles and you weren't, it was more important to shield the camera. The bright torch flares would be enough to ruin the lens on the old cameras we used in those days - they were very different to the compact versions in use today. I had to take a deep breath before picking one up - they weighed a ton - and you could only see what footage was being recorded on a separate monitor that was also pretty heavy. This was connected to the camera by a cable and placed on the floor nearby. I spent many hours sitting on the ground staring at the small black and white screen. If, as happened on one outdoor shoot, the monitor gave up the ghost, you had to trust to luck that the cameraman was getting the shots you wanted and they would piece together neatly in the editing studio.

I heard that when the small, light handicams came into vogue, a television news channel in Canada bought in quite a few, but it caused big problems for their crews. Before, they had been granted instant access to all kinds of places, now they were treated like tourists, and shoved to the back of the crowd as their equipment wasn't recognized as being professional. To solve the problem, they had fake covers made to put round the outside of the small digital cameras, and professional dignity was restored.

In my time I've worked with dozens of cameramen, usually males, due to the large, heavy equipment, and I learned that many of them were dyslexic. While they all had a brilliant ability to 'see' pictures through the lens, and frame subjects in interesting and creative ways, many of them could barely read a script. So I would have to tell them to, for example, take a three second shot of a far-off hill, then a close up of a man working in a field, or a seven second pan of a building and so on. They had no idea of the completed programme, or the story we were trying to tell, but they captured one scene after another to order.

This could make it tricky for the scriptwriter. Sometimes the cameraman would scream that he didn't need to be told how long a shot should be, at others he would stare blankly and say, "Well, how long a shot do you want?"

As different cameramen were hired for individual programmes, it was guesswork as to who you were going to get on any particular day. I soon learned to check with them as to how they wanted directing. Now officially, I wasn't a real director, no special chair for me while I waved my arms about and told dozens of people what to do.

Our crews were usually made up of three people - the cameraman, the gofer who also held the microphone, erected the lights and got things in and out of the van and a third person, who held the script, explained what was coming next and what shots were needed to tell the story or get the message across.

I guess now I've written it down, it does sound like directing, but when there are only three of you, any one of us might have a suggestion to make. But when I went out on shoot, because I had often written the script, and I had done a recce as well, I had the best idea what the client wanted.

Over the years when the crew turned up to shoot, we were met with all kinds of different reactions. Sometimes the client scowled; I think they were expecting just a cameraman with a box brownie. Or, they would grumble if they had to accommodate three or four people, especially if their premises were small, and we all had to crowd into a caravan or a broom closet, if it contained a vital shot which simply *had* to be included in the programme. You could get quite 'up close and personal' with other crew members on occasion.

At other times, they gazed at us in dismay.

"Is that everyone? Where are the rest of the people?"

"No, we're all here."

"Just the three of you?"

They would look so disappointed and I wondered if they expected us to arrive with tracks and dollies and a catering van and a mobile costume and makeup department as well. I did carry a basic kit with me, powder to take the shine off faces, and a bit of blush and even lipstick, but you learned to double up to keep costs down and save time. It was only if the budget was generous that we hired in peripheral specialists, and only if we were featuring a famous presenter. The problem is that too many people watch television these days, and tend to have quite unrealistic expectations.

As for our equipment, there was a large box containing the camera, another box for the lights, which are curiously called blondes and red heads, (possibly because they were painted yellow and red on the back), the tripod, a third box for the sound equipment and we managed to squeeze in the monitor as well. We also had cables and, most importantly the final bag contained our snack bars and drinks. Oh, and I nearly forgot, we also carted around a silver reflector to bounce light onto faces when we were shooting outdoors, and then the small make-up bag.

Personally I think we managed very well, but if our subjects were expecting the production crew required to produce a Hollywood epic, then they were generally disappointed.

Making programmes, or I guess with any artistic venture, it requires teamwork, and you all need to cooperate to produce the best you can. If you upset any one member, then you could easily end up with bad sound, fuzzy pictures or even missing shots. It didn't happen often, but I remember one occasion many years later, when a particular client who had commissioned a programme and was starring in it, had upset the crew members so much, they recorded her from the most unflattering angles, left her partially in the dark in a few shots, and added kilos to her rear end. Unfortunately for her, she was far too busy to come and view the work in progress in edit, and nearly died on the night when she was portrayed on the big screen as the monster from hell.

It was while I was rushing around writing and producing for 'Impact', the SABC Education Department for Informal Education called me in again. I had very little time to spare, but I was not going to turn down the chance of another series and this one would be televised. Once again I was shown into a boardroom and I was in for a shock.

As usual there was an assortment of professionals and educational specialists who were mapping out the subject matter aimed at health educators. One of the ladies thought it would be a great idea to use a child, remove all her clothes, point out to everyone how dirty she was, and then repair the damage. Several round the table nodded in agreement.

Was this for real? How could you do that to any child? How could you expose her to the ridicule of classmates? Wouldn't she be scarred for life?

I was aware that most African children living in both the rural and urban areas had survival skills way beyond those pampered offspring in first world countries. They are tough, but this was taking it a step too far. From my experience the average African was quite fatalistic about life, and would placidly accept situations that those from the so called first world would refuse to put up with. Maybe if you compared their situation with Europe before the First World War, where acceptance was very much the norm and expectations were low, their attitude is more understandable. I suspect that people were quite brutal to each other if it suited their purpose and worrying about upsetting feelings and behaving sensitively was the last thing on their minds.

Normally I sat quietly in these meetings and took notes, but this time I had to speak out. Rather than criticize their approach, I had to come up instantly with a better idea. The only thing I could think of in a hurry was to suggest we used two little girls, both well turned out, one had a clean doll and the other neglected her doll which was always getting sick.

There were frowns all round. I held my breath and prayed they would go for it. I just couldn't see me scripting a scene where we humiliated a child, especially as the filming was going to be in a primary school in one of the local townships, and the 'actors' would be chosen at random and not even paid.

I had a feeling they were not really convinced, but the commissioning manager came to my rescue and backed me up. We would use dolls and maybe her arms and legs could fall off? I wasn't sure quite what that would prove, but I was not about to rock the boat by arguing at this stage.

I took the brief and fled before anyone could change their minds. I never watched the programmes so I have no idea what happened. In fact I don't remember any of the managers ever phoning, faxing or writing to tell me one of my programmes was going out on air. I guess it never occurred to them, it was another reminder that the scriptwriter is always at the bottom of the pecking order.

By day, I was out on shoot, and in the evening I was frantically scripting for both radio and television, which took some mental shifting as I moved from one medium to the other.

'Impact' made a series of programmes for the national electricity supplier Eskom. They were very keen to educate the public about every aspect of the way they generated and supplied electricity. At the same time, they had commissioned another company in Johannesburg to make several training videos for their employees, and I was also involved in writing those, although I only went out on a couple of the shoots.

I remember being more than a little amazed by one entitled 'How to climb a ladder the Eskom way'. This was another reminder of corporate behaviour. If you'd ask me how to climb a ladder, I would have simply said you put one foot on the bottom rung, and then the other foot on the next rung and up you went. Nothing, I learned was that simple.

Before you even began to think about going up a ladder if you were employed by Eskom, you first had to adorn yourself with all kinds of apparatus, clipped on to a harness with all kinds of fastenings, all of which we were required to show in detail.

Looking as if you were about to launch yourself into outer space, you then had to learn exactly where you must place your feet and hands, which way round you needed to hold the rungs, and in which order you moved different limbs to correspond with your ascent.

To follow all the procedures, it took us over twenty minutes to show all these rules, regulations and precautions just to ascend a simple ladder. Then we had to film an extra bit on how to place the ladder against the support in the first place. I had no idea it was that complicated a procedure, and I was shocked to realize that I had been climbing ladders incorrectly my whole life. Isn't it amazing what you learn as you get older?

The Eskom series brought lots of surprises, and for me it was an enormous learning curve. The team and I had been out all day taking shots of the various activities, and I can't remember why we had a shot of erecting pylons in the programme, but we faithfully recorded a large group of hardworking men who were fitting pylons together like enormous pieces of Lego. These shots duly went into the programme, and I was quite pleased with those visuals, as they were interesting and different. Then the big bosses at Eskom saw them and went ballistic.

It transpired that Eskom do not erect pylons, this work is done by imported gangs of Italian workers who specialize in this area. We were roasted for this, but I felt that was quite unfair as no one had told us, so how were we supposed to know? The erectors were dressed exactly the same as the Eskom employees and since we didn't stop to chat to them, none of us had any idea they only spoke Italian.

However, it's not done to argue with your clients even when you feel totally in the right. But we had a bigger problem - how to fill an eighteen second gap in the programme once the Italians had been evicted.

Now I know that eighteen seconds doesn't sound like very much at all, but try sitting and slowly counting up to eighteen while you're staring at a blank wall, and you'll get the picture, or rather you won't.

By now we were up against a very tight deadline and we just didn't have enough spare footage to fill in the gap. You can't insert pastoral scenes or flying birds as cutaways on a programme about electricity. The only thing we could think of doing was to play some of the scenes in slomo, at half or quarter speed. At the rate our Eskom hero climbed his ladder, he would never, ever have got to the top, and I can only hope that all future employees did not learn to climb ladders so slowly!

But the big bosses were happy, and they were the ones who signed the cheques. I was slowly being introduced into the world of corporate propaganda!

Two more Eskom programmes I scripted were a puzzle to me then, and they are still a puzzle to me now. I just couldn't believe what they were telling me and what they wanted to broadcast to the rest of the country. I'm talking about their management techniques. Maybe these were American in origin but who ever came up with the ideas originally must have had a very strange mind indeed.

The first programme was on Participative Management, and in theory it sounded like a great idea. Write down at the beginning of the week all the work you want to have finished by Friday afternoon. So far, so good, but as the end of the week approached, you were then required to fill in a form to record what you had *actually* done and then rate your performance on how well you think you did.

I can go along with that, but now it gets a bit weird. Every Friday after the lunch break, everyone in the department gets together, to compare notes and then rate each other. I sat wide eyed across the desk from my subject specialist in Eskom's personnel department.

"Have I got this straight?" I asked. "I can understand the self assessment, but are you asking all the other employees in your department to rate you as well?"

"That's right."

"Everyone in the department?"

"Yes."

"Not just the managers?"

"No, everyone."

"Sorry if I sound a bit dense, but by everyone, are you including, say, the filing clerks and the tea lady? Everyone?"

"Oh yes, and the cleaning staff. We don't leave anyone out."

I tried not to question how the tea lady could possibly award points for a managerial job not completed when she was probably battling to understand what the heck he should have been doing in the first place. Add to that she wasn't even communicating in her first home language and I didn't see quite how it all fitted together.

"OK, um, and they award you points for what you have done that week?"

"Exactly."

"Would that include people who might want your job, say, people one level below you?"

"Yes, of course."

"But if they were after your position, might they be tempted to be uh, particularly... harsh in their assessments of your performance?"

The Personnel Manager looked completely shocked. "No, of course not!" he replied. "They wouldn't do that!"

Wouldn't they? I wondered. Now I may not have a degree in Psychology, but I think I have a pretty good idea about human nature, and it sounded a very dangerous practice to me. I was also not convinced that my advisor was himself convinced, but this was the official company policy and he was not going to lose his job by questioning anything. I felt rather sorry for him, but I reminded myself that although I might not get a regular pay check every month, at least I did not have to claw my way up the corporate ladder, worrying about who was trying to scrabble up past me and send me flying back to the bottom.

It was not an easy script to write as I had to make it sound upbeat, plausible and enthusiastic. There are many kinds of prostitution!

Their next management programme was on Eskom's Quality Circles. Now this made more sense. It was an idea which first began in Japan after World War II and then the Americans took an interest when they saw how quickly Japan improved the quality of their manufacturing.

These Circles consist of a few employees, again right from middle management to the cleaners and the tea ladies, to discuss problems they have in doing their day to day work. They talk about how these difficulties might be resolved and how working conditions and methods might be improved. Their recommendations are then sent to senior management to discuss and hopefully, implement.

I was enthusiastic about writing this programme, it was an easy concept to get across on paper and I agreed with the principles, which always helps. After a couple of minor changes, they signed off the script and it was time to pre-produce and plan the shooting schedule. I suggested their head office, called Megawatt Park, on the northern outskirts of Johannesburg.

"No, we want to show a 'typical' Quality Circle."

"So, what do we need for a 'typical' Quality Circle?"

"Men, women, black people of course, and an Indian as well."

"Of course - how silly of me, it must be representative of the population as a whole."

"Yes, we should have a coloured person too, that would be perfect. We want to show a 'typical' one."

(In South Africa, 'coloured' refers to those people who are descended from the Malay people who were brought to the Cape to work on the farms centuries earlier).

"So you *don't* have a 'typical' one here in Megawatt Park?"

"No. I will have to make some enquiries," said our Eskom specialist, "and then we can arrange for you to shoot there."

A few days later, the phone rang and the Eskom man told us in excited tones that he had found the perfect Quality Circle, and he would make all the bookings for us to go and film them.

"Great," I said. "Where are they based?"

"Thabazimbi."

"Where?"

"Thabazimbi."

"Uh, where is that?"

"Northern Transvaal."

119

"Not in this province then?"

"No."

"How far is it from Johannesburg to Thabazimbi?" I asked.

"Oh, it's only about two hundred kilometres."

I glanced at the map on the wall. Bloody hell, Thabazimbi was not that far from the South African border with Botswana! My first thought was that this was going to blow the budget right out of the water, and told him so.

No problem, he informed me, he would arrange the flights.

Now I was interested I love flying, especially if someone else was paying for the tickets.

On the due date we piled into the crew van and drove to the airport. I must admit it hadn't occurred to me that we wouldn't be flying in the planes I was more used to, which took you from Europe to the southern tip of Africa. The plane that was waiting for us on the tarmac resembled a large mosquito, and I wondered if we would be able to get the three of us, and the equipment inside.

Eventually we took off and I was amazed to see that we flew just a little above roof top height most of the way.

We landed at our destination on a rather bumpy grass runway and were collected in an Eskom car. They blanched at the sight of such a large crew and all the camera gear, and had to use the phone in the hut at the side of runway to ask them to send another car. Even a large corporation did not know what to expect when it came to the size of the crew.

The shoot went off very well, but I was not convinced that this Quality Circle had been in operation for very long. To begin with, they didn't seem to know each other's names. The black tea lady looked most uncomfortable, and the coloured floor sweeper didn't open his mouth once. To make matters worse, no one seemed to have any problems with their area of work, and therefore no suggestions as to how it could be improved. But we did the best we could and by five in the evening, it was a wrap.

They gave us a brief tour of the power station and added some impressive statistics about the electricity output and the number of homes, offices, businesses and manufacturing outlets it supplied through its air cooling systems.

By now, the gofer and sound guy, one and the same, was totally fed up and when the clients suggested they treat us to a meal at their brand new, drive-by roadside restaurant, he rather rudely answered for all of us and said he wanted to get back to civilization. He'd had enough of the rural backwater, and he could eat any day at a roadside restaurant in Johannesburg.

Our delightful hosts were quite taken aback, as this new eatery was the talk of the town and at the top of their tourist attractions. It was probably their *only* tourist attraction!

I hastily tried to smooth things over as they drove us back to the plane and we all piled into the aircraft again.

Fate has a habit of getting her own back. When the same sound gofer was doing his two year army service, guess where he was stationed for six months? Yes, in the army camp in Thabazimbi! He hated it!

A few months later, I needed shots of air pollution, and once again, the Film Library charges were way outside our budget. I phoned one of my contacts in Megawatt Park and explained my dilemma.

"No problem, we have lots of pictures of our plants polluting the atmosphere. Pop on over and choose as many as you like."

I was amazed, we had made numerous programmes for them extolling their clean air policies, and we'd broadcast them on national television, was that just another piece of propaganda?

10 THE TOKOLOSHE AND THE CAMERMAN

The next few programmes I did were about food. It just shows how low 'some' money-grabbing scriptwriters will sink, when they agree to write about the efficacy of low cholesterol foods, condemning the consumption of potatoes in the diet at the beginning of the week; while at the end of the same week, they are extolling the virtues of potato chips, listing all the vitamins and minerals they contain which are excellent for your health. In fact *huge* quantities of potato chips are essential to a well balanced diet I was informed.

I'll never forget my interview with the chief lady of the chip company. I simply couldn't get over how enthusiastic she was about her product, and when I say enthusiastic, I mean *really* enthusiastic. For crying out loud, they're only a form of cooked potato for heaven's sake! She was particularly thrilled since they'd just composed a new dance for their marketing mascot to introduce the new chutney flavoured range. 'OK,' I thought, 'that's mildly interesting!'

Apparently it was more than interesting for the chip lady, and I began to think she was ready to launch herself into orbit with the excitement of it all.

I dutifully took down all the information and she was one of those nice, easy clients who was happy with the first draft.

However I was not as happy when we went to shoot the programme. The factory was absolutely filthy! I guess it must be impossible to keep a place spotless when you have huge vats of boiling oil and raw potatoes having their skins ground off.

As we attempted to focus the camera on areas that were more salubrious, I thought, not for the first time, about all those clever, inventive people who design all the machinery to print packages, blow air into them, fill them with stuff, and then self seal them; and we have no idea who they are, unlike the famous football kickers and tuneless warblers. But stand by a production line for a few moments and you can't help but marvel at the intricacies and engineering skills involved in mass preparation and packaging.

Our enthusiastic client was just as enthusiastic about the finished programme and, despite her over the top reactions, she was one of the nicest clients I ever wrote for.

At the other end of the scale, the SABC actually flew me down to Durban to meet up with the people who made low-fat margarine. I didn't get into the factory this time, but I returned north-west with my head stuffed full of facts about fat cells and heart attacks and the other terrible things that could happen to you if you so much as looked at a slab of butter, a block of cheese or a potato chip.

These clients were poles apart from the chip lady as they appeared positively terrified of eating the wrong foods, abusing their bodies or failing to keep in the peak of fitness at all times. They gave me the impression they lived on their nerves, were fighting off stomach ulcers and were possibly heading for nervous breakdowns. The word Valium kept popping into my head, (this was in pre-Prozac days), and as I cheerfully bought a large packet of chips at the airport, I decided that life was more fun if you fed your fat cells to keep them happy.

We made another series of programmes for a different photographic film processing company, rivals to the first bunch, and they wanted to include the history of photography. I had a great time with this one as the budget was large enough for me to hire costumes and set up scenes with role-playing.

It began with a couple of cavemen, suitably attired to show that before pictures, people had to use words to describe what they had seen. Caveman One was trying to describe a mammoth, using grunts and sign language, while our talented in-house graphic artist drew cartoons to show what Caveman Two understood from the gestures - all the wrong kinds of animals, of course.

The series manager Bob, who'd been so helpful to me at the beginning, was well known in the dramatic field and he also got involved on camera on this one. We had him in various roles to show the passing of the centuries. We found a quiet road for him to walk down while we shot him in medieval costume, and nearly caused an accident when a driver came round the corner and didn't see the camera, but he did see Bob dressed in weird clothes doing some very strange sweeping and hopping motions in the middle of the road.

The next day, we noticed a perfect doorway of just the right period for the 18th century shots. He was to walk up to it, knock and then we would fade out before the door was opened. It would be funnier to say that some irate homeowner dressed in jeans and a sweat shirt opened the door and shouted at us, but luckily, no one was home. We had not asked permission to use the doorway.

For the final shot, we got a crew in Durban to show people splashing about in the Indian Ocean geared up in old fashioned bathing costumes, and apparently that drew quite a crowd of puzzled spectators.

When it came to locations, we often used the homes and gardens belonging to the office staff or the crew members. I quite liked the idea of my neighbours seeing a television crew van draw up outside my house, unload all the equipment and disappear inside. It's an excellent way of showing off without having to say a word.

So when we needed a shot of two youngsters having breakfast in a domestic situation, I quickly offered them my house and my children. I also hoped that it would raise my own status with my daughters. They took no notice at all of any of the programmes I had been involved with on radio or television. Like the rest of the viewing public, they only ever concentrated on the celebrities and stars on the screen.

I would point out that if the lighting crew switched off the lights, the sound people went on strike, the scriptwriter forgot to give them any words to say and the director didn't tell them what to do, how wonderful would these famous people look then? It was like talking to a brick wall. Mind you, I can hardly blame them - star worship is firmly established now all over the world. Perhaps it's a throw back from the days when to be an actress was barely a step above working as a prostitute. It took the King of England's libido to finally change the mindset. But maybe we have now gone to the other extreme.

The crew traipsed into our house, set up the lights, camera and sound gear, and in a couple of hours it was all over. It was gratifying to see people peeping through their curtains and walking past the house ever so slowly. I was pleased, that is until I got the next electricity bill - it was astronomical! I had not realized just how much power the studio lighting drained off the national grid. I was asked several more times if they could film at my house and the answer was always "No!"

Years later, when we filmed in private houses in the townships, I always budgeted in extra money to allow us to pay the owners something to cover the cost of the electricity we used.

Another programme that I remember very well was for an organization which had set up offices in one of the black townships which ring Johannesburg. It was called 'The Get Ahead Foundation', formed to assist fledgling businessmen with grants, loans and information to help them grow their businesses and provide further employment. They had a success story they wanted us to highlight, so I drove into Alexandra on a recce with my favourite cameraman, Reggie.

The star of our show was a cheerful and friendly man called Shadrack Khopotse who manufactured asbestos pool pump covers. He had quite a sizeable workshop with at least twenty workers who were all busy pouring a thick liquid material mixed with asbestos into large moulds. When the shapes were dry they were turned out, and placed upside down over swimming pool pumps to make them look neat and tidy.

While I was admiring the set up and smiling at the workers, Reggie was having a fit, he was quite beside himself.

"What's the matter?" I asked him.

"We can't film all this!" he exclaimed.

"Why not?"

"Haven't you noticed all this asbestos flying about in the air?" Actually, I hadn't, but he did have a point. I felt quite sorry for our friendly proprietor as Reggie berated him for his lack of health and safety standards. He was trying to explain that a factory like this was very dangerous to the health of his workers and he must provide protective clothing.

The owner listened attentively, while eying the workers who were sidling over to eavesdrop, at the same time trying to contain their excitement about appearing on national television. The due date was set for filming and I rushed off to write the script.

When we returned to the pool pump cover workshop I was amazed at the transformation. It had been scrubbed clean from top to bottom, and everything was in perfect order, including the workers. Each one was now enveloped in a bright, shiny, yellow coat with a matching fisherman's hat and wore a regulation face mask. All you could see were their eyes, and it was impossible to tell one from another, or even if they were male or female. If they thought they were going to be recognizable on television, they were going to be severely disappointed.

Our delightful host had explained to us that previously, before the 'Get Ahead' crowd had helped facilitate his loan, his old pick-up truck only worked in third and fourth gears. Since there was quite a steep incline on the road out of Alexandra Township, he was forced to stop at the bottom, unload all the completed pool pump covers, leave them at the bottom, turn the vehicle round and reverse up the hill. Then he had to walk down, collect the covers and carry them back to the truck parked at the top of the hill. As he earnestly explained, this took a lot of time, and he risked having his truck hijacked as he walked to and fro.

I thought it unlikely that thieves could successfully steal a car without first and second gears - it wouldn't have been easy to make a quick getaway. I thought it more likely that they would make off with the new pool pump covers.

I remember Reggie being in a very bad mood on that shoot, and as he was our main cameraman, and was also doing the presentation live to camera, I simply did as I was told and left the organizing to him. I liked working with Reggie, but the only annoying fault he had was insisting I use the clapperboard between shots. This was a fiddle, since on some occasions we were down to only two in the crew and I would have to keep jumping up and down every time he rolled the camera. There were more important things for me to do, like set up the next shot.

After showing Mr Khopotse's old and new transportation delivering pool pump covers, (luckily the brand new pick-up possessed all four gears plus a fifth); and after recording the activity in the factory, we then moved on to the offices of 'The Get Ahead Foundation'. I can't remember now why we used a makeshift office, but we were taken up some stairs behind one of the local bars and invited to use a room, which we could pretend was used by 'Get Ahead.'

It was a very small room with one large table and two chairs. The bar owner was really helpful and appeared in the doorway carrying a spare telephone and a telephone directory, explaining it would help to make it look more like an office.

Reggie just grunted, and to make space for the tripod, he shoved the table nearer the wall. There was an ominous creaking sound and one of the table legs fell off. Reggie swore - well I think he did as his first language was Sotho - but I could tell from his face he was extremely angry.

The Foundation's representative came in and Reggie put him on one of the chairs behind the desk which was now tilting at a precarious angle. Despite the poor man's attempt to hold it in place with his knee, we were forced to use the telephone directory to wedge the table against the wall so that it was more or less level.

Our troubles didn't stop there. When Shadrack, our pool pump man, came in to re-enact his initial interview, Reggie placed him on the chair on the opposite side of the desk, but it broke too, depositing our star on the floor.

By now Reggie was in a really, really, foul mood. I raced downstairs to the bar, but they didn't have any chairs we could borrow, and the best I could do was to return with a couple of red plastic Coca-Cola crates instead. Unfortunately, these were not really high enough and our star was now perched precariously with his nose just level with the top of the table. The addition of a third crate had him looking down at his interviewer from a lofty height, but Reggie muttered that he would adjust the camera angles as necessary. He then noticed that the table, now minus the telephone directory was, apart from the phone, completely bare. Remember, we were using the phone book to help prop up the desk, so he reached over and grabbed my clipboard and pen, ripped the script to shreds and scattered it across the table. Finally, we were now ready to start filming.

By now our cast of two were well and truly rattled, and when Reggie told the 'Get Ahead' man to make a phone call he was totally bemused. He reached out and held up the telephone cord to show it was not connected to anything.

"How can I use this phone?" he asked. "It is not working."

"Yes, we know that. You are going to pretend to make a telephone call," snarled Reggie. "Dial in some numbers and then pretend you are talking on the phone."

The bemused man punched in several numbers while Reggie recorded a close up shot of his fingers on the phone. Then he asked him to repeat the action again, while he prepared to film a medium shot of the same thing. Our interviewer was now totally confused.

"But I've just done that," he moaned.

"Yes, I know but I want you to do it again."

"Why, did I not do it right?"

"Yes, it was fine but I need it again."

Dutifully the man punched the buttons a second time and sat and waited.

"Now talk to the person you have telephoned," instructed Reggie.

"There is no one there," replied our hapless actor.

I thought at this point that Reggie was about to blow a fuse, and then I suddenly noticed there was a calendar on the wall depicting a luscious, naked blonde, licking her lips while offering everyone a can of beer. Swiftly I leaned across and removed it. How had we not noticed it before?

It seemed to take hours until Reggie was finally satisfied

with the footage he had captured and I breathed a sigh of relief as we exited the wrecked office and headed for the crew van. Our next stop was a house in the suburbs to show one of our main star's pool pump covers being installed.

Yes, it had been one of those days and it continued, because when we arrived at the agreed house the owner wasn't at home, so we sat outside and waited for her and for Shadrack who was to drive over in his new pick-up with the cover.

I hesitated to ask Reggie why he was in such a bad mood, but I didn't need to. He was so full of anger that it all came tumbling out. He wanted to know how easy it would be for him to go and work in England.

"But why would you want to do that? You're one of the best cameramen in Johannesburg, and you have work coming out of your ears!" I knew that the industry was paying top rates for crew members of Reggie's calibre. Not only was he an excellent cameraman, he could also speak several African languages, and that made it easier and quicker to set up scenes and get the cooperation we needed, though Reggie much preferred to use English.

"I need to get away from my family," he told me. "Every payday it's the same. They are all waiting at my door before I even get out of the car, and they all want money. It's for school fees, or new shoes, or rent, food, transport. They all want money, my money."

"Oh, that must be difficult. Can't you say no?"

"How can I? It's in our culture to share with family. But they just sit around doing nothing all day while I am working long hours, and then they come to ask for my money. I am tired of sharing. How am I going to get ahead and find a better house, and pay lobola (bride price) for a wife, and send my children to good schools, if my relatives take all my money every month?"

I could see he had a problem. It's one of those clashes between the modern world and the traditional African way of life, and it's something many of us were not even aware of. Those young Africans who had worked hard at school, went on to tertiary education and got well-paid jobs, were also being held back from enjoying the rewards that should come with their new status.

"And they are always wanting me to take them places in my car," Reggie grumbled. "It costs me a lot of money for the petrol, but they just say I can afford it."

I felt privileged that Reggie chose to share his problems with me, and on the many shoots we did together we would often try and put the world to rights while he gave me an amazing insight into life for him in his township, and the pressures and jealousy he encountered from those who were ready to take free hand outs from him while making no effort to help themselves. I have lost touch with Reggie, although I did hear that he went to London, but I think he returned to Johannesburg a few years later.

I know that a lot has been written about the evils of apartheid, and it was evil, but the media industry was one where we all worked together in total harmony, and no one was aware of the colour of your skin. You either had the talent or you didn't, and those who were good at what they did were appreciated regardless of where they came from.

I had previously refused to go and live in South Africa as I did not approve of separate development and banning one race from using public facilities, or forbidding them from living anywhere they chose to. Reggie didn't have the choice of moving out to a white suburb, and similarly, I did not have the opportunity to live in a black township. It shows how well we worked together, as I was always happy to go into any black area with Reggie when we were on shoot.

Although most of the apartheid laws were still on the

books, and officially we were in a state of emergency, in the movie making business and in the arts world, we were all working together sharing our passion for making the best programmes we could.

However, having said that, there were many instances which demonstrated ignorance about other cultures. A prime example of this was a drinks company which flighted their advertisements on all the commercial channels. It showed a group of accountants sitting at a bar, and they offer the barman a free drink. The barman is so astonished he disappears behind the counter in a dead faint. The message intimated the alcohol was so good it put you in an excellent mood, even to the extent that tight fisted accountants would pay out their hard earned cents to treat the barman. A quiet giggle from most Europeans and that was that.

The message on the other side of the culture divide was "don't drink this product whatever you do! It kills you! Look what happened to that poor barman." Sales fell through the floor.

Another example was the couple lying in bed.

Husband: "I have brought you something for your headache dear," as he holds up a well-known brand of pain killers.

Wife: "But I don't have a headache darling."

Husband: "Oh, good!" Husband smiles and then snuggles down and puts the light out.

This was equally confusing to the Africans. What does having a headache got to do with lying in bed? And why did they turn the lights out? African women, from a man's point of view, were much better trained.

While I'm on the subject of cameramen (I strayed off the point a little), I'll jump ahead a few years to when I had my own production company and I hired another favourite cameraman called Subisiso. He was also a fascinating mix of the old and the new world. Because the crew was often away for two or three weeks together on shoot several times a year, we got to know each other very well.

Subisiso told me about his boyhood growing up as a young Zulu in Kosi Bay, a small town up near the Mozambique border. One of the greatest influences in his life was seeing tribal justice in action. When the townsfolk caught a youth stealing, he was stripped naked and forced to run down the main street while the bystanders threw rocks at him, or beat him with sticks. From that day on, Subisiso vowed never to steal anything, or break the law. Even years later when his car accidently hit an unoccupied stationary vehicle, he left his name and address under the windscreen wiper for the owner to contact him so he could pay for the damage. That is not a story you hear very often in Africa.

An incident I do remember was one morning in Kimberley where we were all staying in a guest house, and Subisiso came in to breakfast as white as a sheet. He grabbed my shoulder and in a loud whisper, begged me to change rooms with him.

"Well I don't mind, but why? What's the problem with your room?" I had always believed in taking it in turns to choose both the room and where we were going to eat in the evening, and Subisiso had chosen his room only the night before.

"I was visited by the Tokoloshe last night," he hissed.

In Zulu mythology, the Tokoloshe is a dwarf-like water sprite, a mischievous and evil spirit that can become invisible by drinking water. It's called up by malevolent people to cause trouble for others and can cause illness or even death. It preys on people while they're sleeping and is known to rape women and bite off people's toes in the night. The only way to get rid of it is to call in the sangoma or witch doctor who, for a price, will banish it from the area.

133

Most of us had heard about the Tokoloshe because in every maid's quarters or, *kaya* (I believe they now refer to them as the 'accommodation for the domestic maintenance assistants'), the moment they move into a new *kaya*, they are off to find bricks to put under the legs of the bed. This is a protection against the Tokoloshe.

So I was well aware of the fear that Subisiso had about being visited in the night by this evil spirit and I agreed to swap rooms. I must admit to sleeping just as well in my new room, but what surprised me was Subisiso was a well-educated young man. He'd graduated after studying Video Technology for three years at Durban Technikon and was a very active member of his Christian church.

To add to the mixture of cultures, Subisiso had three children with three different partners who, according to him did not know about each other. His son and daughters were passed around family members like parcels. They lived for a few months in different towns and attended different schools each time.

One of the unhappiest moments of his life was when Subisiso's father failed to attend his graduation ceremony, even though he had sent him the taxi fare and arranged to host him in his flat in Durban. I never had the courage to ask him about his relationship with his own children whom he rarely saw, and who didn't appear to have a very stable childhood. I'm not sure he even noticed the parallels between his failed relationship with his father and his own absentee fatherhood.

Up until that time I'd refused to believe that medical doctors trained overseas would still visit their local *sangoma*, or witch doctor, for pills and potions to attract a woman or counteract a spell which had been put on them, but I guess those stories may well be true. Even today, Africa is a fascinating mix of old and new.

11 NATION BUILDING

There is a lot of suspicion about new ideas, and I was called in to a company called Cashbuild to help change mindsets amongst their staff. Cashbuild was a huge concern, selling building materials throughout the country, from wheelbarrows, to bricks, cement, tools, corrugated sheeting and so on. In order to protect their employees they had introduced a pension scheme, where they kept back two Rand a week (less than a dollar), to which they added four Rand and invested it for their employees, so when they either left the company or retired they would have a lump sum.

There were near-riots outside their warehouses and head office when the employees discovered they were being short changed. As far as they were concerned, the fat cat managers at Cashbuild were keeping the money for themselves and stealing it from the poor workers.

So the top brass decided to make a video to explain in simple language exactly how the scheme worked, and that is where I came in. I'm not sure what effect the final product had, but my early training in teaching a concept step by step, certainly came in useful, and Cashbuild is still alive and profitable today.

Later that year, I met another man who impressed me deeply. I went in to meet the editor of the Sowetan Newspaper in downtown Johannesburg. I know many of the people I mixed with socially avoided this area like the plague, and spent their leisure time in the game parks and the northern suburbs, but whether it was because my work out on shoot had taken me to most parts of the cities, or foolhardiness, or just plain ignorance, I didn't think twice when I drove in to the city.

Aggrey Klaaste was dressed impeccably in a dark suit and rose to welcome me into his office. He ordered coffee and then explained some background to the programme he wanted to make. He told me about his passion for the concept he introduced called 'Nation Building'. He asked if I had seen the bumper stickers. Yes, I had, but not thought to ask what it was all about.

"I am going to America soon," he continued, "and I want to take a video with me to show people what 'Nation Building' is all about. I, for one, am ashamed to be black."

Inwardly I groaned. I hoped he wasn't going to complain about the evils of apartheid. I wanted to plead ignorance and explain that I had no part in it, and I didn't agree with it either - being relatively new in South Africa I didn't even have the right to vote. But his next words took me totally by surprise.

"Do you know what percentage of the prison population in America is black?" he asked me.

"Uh, no, I have no idea."

"80%. And what percentage of drug takers is black?"

"Uh, no, no I don't."

"75%."

"Um," I was not sure how to respond.

"And the figures for blacks unemployed in America are around 78%."

I had no idea what Mr Klaaste was trying to tell me, and I think he must have noticed the look on my face as he smiled, removed his glasses to wipe them on a tissue and said "This was my reason for starting 'Nation Building', it is urging people to do things for themselves. It is about time we, as a nation and a race, learned that we are not here to receive handouts and bleat about the past. We must develop a work ethic and get up off our backsides."

To say I was shocked is an understatement. This was absolutely amazing coming from a successful black businessman who I thought had every right to be angry with the way the government ran South Africa. I sat enthralled that whole afternoon as Aggrey Klaaste told me how he'd been born in Kimberley, one of eight children. They'd later moved to Johannesburg where his father was a clerk on the goldmines. Aggrey was one of the last to graduate from WITS University before it was closed to blacks. He now lived in Soweto, the largest black township near Johannesburg, but told me that his children went to private schools, being chauffeured out daily, but sometimes, due to the unrest they had to sleep over in the white areas with friends.

He said as soon as they repealed the last of the laws, he would be moving out of Soweto into the suburbs. He felt a little guilty because there was a need for leaders in the townships to guide the people, but he had to think of his own family. He felt he was playing his part by creating and promoting 'Nation Building'. He said if the black population in America was still at the bottom of the heap, even after they'd had access to a good education and a reasonable standard of living for over two centuries, then there was need for a radical mindset change. If the black man in South Africa wanted to make the country great, he would have to stop moaning and start working.

"We have been blessed with a wealth of minerals, a long coastline with access to the world, and a vast market for our goods north of the continent. We have everything we need to succeed, except the way we think."

Aggrey Klaaste died in 2004, but he is remembered for his efforts at promoting inter-racial reconciliation, despite the fact that he had been imprisoned for 9 months by the white government. He was voted 58th in the Top 100 South Africans, and was one of those people who made a great and lasting impression on me, and who I admired tremendously. I took extra time and effort in writing the script for 'Nation Building'. I wasn't involved in the production, but when I saw the finished programme, I was proud to have been a part of it.

When the 'Impact' series started there were two fulltime sales people who would canvass companies over the phone and then go and visit them to persuade them to buy an insert. It was only then, as one of the scriptwriters I would visit them again to research their products and new innovations then write the script.

For one reason or another both the sales staff left, and we were getting very thin on the ground with programmes to produce. This is a terrifying feeling when you know you have to provide thirty minutes a week of television come hell or high water. The in-house staff were incredibly creative, putting together a science corner each week, with one of the subject specialists on camera asking questions such as "Is it better to run or walk when it's raining if you're trying to stay dry?"

They also hit on the idea of repeating some of the earlier programmes 'by popular request'. A total lie of course, so if you ever hear this comment on radio or television, you will know exactly what it means - we have run out of new stuff and are being forced to repeat earlier programmes and inserts!

I was getting nervous. If we failed to deliver each Friday, then I was out of work. Sitting in the production office I picked up the phone one day to follow a couple of leads the departed sales lady had left on the desk. Much to my surprise the company invited me along for a chat. The next day I ignored the usual jeans and t-shirt, rummaged at the back of my wardrobe for a long neglected suit left over from teaching days and, armed with my briefcase, set off for down town Pretoria.

I made two sales. One for an office machine company - where I learned that the fax machine had been invented in the 1840s by a Scotsman - and one other programme, the subject of which escapes me. I will have to continue to write very fast before that fact, along with so many others, disappears into my memory banks, never to surface again!

A large German textile manufacturing company commissioned a programme about an innovative new fabric and this time I was not involved in either the scripting, or the production, but simply asked to book the voice over and direct the recording. In those days a small monitor was set up in the sound booth and the artist would read from the script as the programme was played through up on the screen, and the sound recorded onto large reels of audio tape. This way, the voice elaborated on the visuals and everything would be in sync.

These days the narration is recorded separately mixed later on the computer and then laid down as a separate layer in the final mix.

Back then, if the voice over artist made a mistake, coughed or sneezed, the sound engineer would stop him, wind back the tape and overlay the correct version. So there was very little I had to do except check to see that the correct words were read and he or she didn't miss out a sentence or two. I would also keep an eye on the monitor to check that it was all in sync, with the right words to the right picture.

I was told to choose a good artist, and I thought back to my early days at the SABC and I remembered Colin Fish, who had been kind, helpful and encouraging, and offering him the job seemed a good way of saying thank you. I think by then he had retired from the SABC, and people in the media world are always in need of extra cash. He was very happy to come in, and we had a friendly chat over a cup of coffee while they set up the booth.

All went well for the first half page, and then it all began to fall apart.

"The textiles that was put together in order to produces them clothes...." read Colin, before he came storming out of the booth. "I'm not reading this rubbish!" he exclaimed. "What's wrong with you lot? Can't you write proper English?"

"Look, I'm sorry Colin, but this programme was sponsored by the CEO of this company and he's German."

"I don't care if he's from bloody Mars! This isn't correct English!"

"Yes, I know that, you know that, but he insisted on writing the script, and when we pointed out to him that we say things a little differently, he got very irate and said he wanted it left exactly the way he wrote it."

"I'm not ruining my good name by publicly reading out that rubbish. I have my reputation to consider," Colin was furious.

I groaned. We were up against a tight deadline here as our German client had been particularly difficult to work with. I knew that all the titles, including the voice over credits, which already included Colin's name, were completed. Once they had 'final packaged' this week's episode, I just hoped it wouldn't be me driving at over 120 kilometres down the freeway, to deliver the programme to the SABC to meet our deadline.

I tried again. "How about you read it in a German accent?" Not a good idea, Colin Fish was of the old school and he still had early memories of the last World War. Telling him the client was German hadn't helped matters either.

I begged and pleaded with him until at last, reluctantly, he read most of the script, correcting only in places where the English grammar was so appalling even I winced.

I also had a hard time when I persuaded a popular star to appear on our insert about microwave cooking. We were at a social gathering and I caught him unaware after a few drinks. He was so well-known I knew his appearance would add value to the programme and I couldn't wait to tell the production staff on Monday morning.

Three days later when it was time to record the insert, I had a hard time getting hold of Paul, and an even harder time persuading him to come to the studios. He'd had a long, hard think in the meantime and realized that appearing in an 'Impact' programme was only a fraction above the humiliating appearance of showing up in a television commercial.

I have to thank Paul as he did turn up, and he did play his part well, but he gave the crew a very hard time. Microwave ovens were fairly new then, and he kept questioning the facts, refusing to believe that the food cooked from the inside out, and why it seemed that some containers stayed cool, while the food inside them was hot.

I stayed well out of the way and only popped into the studio to collect his invoice and hand him a bottle of his favourite wine just before he left.

One of the pitfalls of writing for television is the budget.

A few months earlier in one script, I had included a shot of a rocket going into space. I don't remember the subject now, but when they questioned me, I assured them that it was a vital scene and must be kept in the programme.

"And are we supposed to just nip over to Cape Kennedy and take a quick shot?" snarled the Production Secretary.

I knew better! "No, you can buy these shots. Didn't you know?" I felt I had enough production experience to know about these things by now, and she was new to the job, fresh out of film school. "I've bought in lots of shots for the 'Impact' series before, and they were well within budget."

"Fine," she spat at me. "Fine, if you're buying locally here in South Africa, do you have any idea how much the Americans charge for stock footage? And for something like a moon shot?"

Ah, no, I didn't. I had no idea. Humbly, I apologized.

Another client I upset was also German. I can't remember why he called me in - it wasn't for an 'Impact' insert - but I do remember asking him what his shooting budget was. These are usually costed out to give the scriptwriter an idea of what can and can't be included, and rates are quoted by the minute.

If you have a production budget of several thousand per minute, then you can include aerial shots, use a boom camera, hire in tracks and dollies and pay to have music specially written for the occasion. A few pennies or cents a minute and you get a cheap, nondescript, amateur presenter in his own clothes, with a blackboard and a piece of chalk!

There are all stages in between, of course, but this German client went quite purple in the face.

"Vat, yer want to know vat I make?" he screamed at me. "Is none of yer business, it is not for yer to know."

"No, no you don't understand. I'm not asking about your profit, but how much you have earmarked for the budget so that I can...."

"I 'ear you very well. You are nosey, no?"

I tried again. "Can you afford to hire a helicopter, or should I keep it simple and write in only a couple of locations? Or maybe you..." I could see from his face that I was not getting my point across.

I didn't get the job.

But it was always important to find out before you wrote the script what you could and couldn't include. It was no good writing in lots of exciting stuff if you then had to go back to the drawing board and start all over again. I was reminded of Jack's remarks about casts the size of Ben Hur, and that was only for radio.

But things seldom stay the same. For one reason or another, the SABC canned the 'Impact' series and suddenly, we were all looking for work.

12 INSERTS OF ALL SORTS

I was seriously worried for a week or so, but then my friendly managers at the SABC called me in and offered me a couple more radio series. One of these fell under the Informal Adult Education umbrella, and we decided that this would take the form of a presenter and a medical expert, who was supposed to be a nurse, and they would answer letters sent in by the public on various related topics.

Of course, for the first few programmes we didn't *have* any letters, so there are no prizes for guessing who had to write those as well.

With a map of South Africa on one side of the desk and a telephone book for suggesting names on the other, I wrote out their imaginary letters, and in the resulting dialogue I magically solved all their problems.

This was all going fine until the day the letters *really began to roll in.* While my actors had been discussing bed wetting or temper tantrums or not liking vegetables, it was not these issues which were bothering the listeners. Once again, I was too firmly entrenched in my own culture. These problems were quite different.

I sought medical advice, and discovered that the symptoms and problems people were describing were indications of brain tumours, of severe mental retardation or radically arrested physical development. The cries for help were heartbreaking, and this was one project where I would not let my defences down and make even the gentlest joke. The whole series took on dark undertones, and writing five episodes a week for thirteen weeks took a heavy toll on me.

Every now and again, the SABC would go off into the townships and ask people what they thought of the radio programmes that were being broadcast. This wasn't just to find out about those dreaded ratings on which the balance of a whole series would be in jeopardy if too few listeners tuned in. No - this was done to evaluate the effects the educational programmes were having, and if they were making a difference in people's lives.

They returned time and time again to Auckland Park with rave reviews and lots of praise for what they were sending out over the airwaves - in fact maybe a little too much praise. So someone hit on the bright idea of recording the signature tunes to a few programmes and asking people to identify them.

Now it was a different story. They were met with blank stares and shrugs as the people battled to match the music with the correct programme. The people in high office had forgotten the golden rule that it is very bad manners in African culture to give bad news, so of course when they had been asked initially they were full of praise, even though they were lying through their teeth. They were simply being polite.

So it was reassuring to know that when the real letters poured in for this latest series, there *were* people out there listening and interacting.

Since a couple of my SABC managers had been told from on high they must spread the work around a little more, several of the companies producing programmes for other series were steered in my direction and urged to use me to write their scripts. I was not going out on shoots as often, but I continued to scribble full time.

A company in Johannesburg was commissioned to produce inserts for 'Good Morning South Africa', and one of the topics was 'What to do in an emergency', based on the Reader's Digest book of the same name. How many of us would rush to look up instructions in a book at a time like that I'm not sure, but remembering the visuals on television might help.

This was a fascinating series on how to protect yourself against all kinds of dangers. I cheerfully wrote about what to do if a bomb went off, a gang rushed into the shopping mall guns blazing, how to cope with snake bites, electrocution, drowning and so on and so on. Any emergency you could possibly think of, we had it covered. The only information I was told to take out was the danger of letter bombs, as that particular form of terrorism had not been used frequently in South Africa, and it was not to be encouraged.

By the end of the series, I was quite an expert at getting myself out of trouble and in the future, on more than one occasion, I flung myself to the ground to avoid being shot. It did occur to me, however, that we might just have passed on a few suggestions to the would-be freedom fighters/terrorists who were still demanding political equality.

More inserts poured in for GMSA and some were quite bizarre, like towing icebergs from Antarctica to Cape Town to supply fresh water. It was calculated that by 2020, the 'Mother City' would not be able to supply potable water for all its citizens. Some bright spark had thought of popping a large plastic bag over a passing lump of ice, then hijacking it with a lasso and towing it to the base of Table Mountain. Apparently there was also talk of taking one to Dubai.

Marion Island lies off the coast of South Africa, and when I wrote about it, I thought it was quite close to the mainland. Now, I discover that it is much closer to Antarctica. It's only 19 kilometres long and 12 wide, but it is a haven for wild life and a year-round research team is stationed there in the national park. The island was suffering from a surfeit of rats, so they decided to introduce a couple of cats to eliminate the rats and protect the rare birds and other endangered species.

Yes, I'm sure you're one jump ahead of me here. The moggies were very successful, too successful in fact. After they had chomped their way through the rat population, they turned their sights on the rare and endangered bird population.

At the same time, they took excellent care of their own population development by breeding more like rabbits than cats, creating another problem - how were they going to cull most of the felines and sterilize the rest?

I loved learning and writing about so many interesting new facts and researching in my encyclopaedias (of which you might remember, I had quite a few) or perhaps I am just terribly nosey.

I learned about distance education, which was a lot more complicated than I had suspected, since it involved preparing all the instruction books, liaising with lecturers for marking and arranging exam venues. Again, I remember feeling more than a little uncomfortable as I was taken on a guided tour of their printing works where I was introduced to the elderly workers who paid me far more respect and reverence than I deserved, and all because I represented the 'Great God of Television'.

There was an International Round the World Yacht Race taking place, and each of the competitors had been asked to keep a diary of what they saw, particularly the rubbish, the sea birds and other creatures they encountered on their travels.

The insert series was called 'Ocean Watch' and the information they reported back was horrendous. They saw hundreds and hundreds of plastic bags and other household rubbish bobbing about on the waves, even in the middle of the Pacific Ocean. There were empty plastic bottles and waterlogged flotsam and jetsam of every kind. There were also abandoned containers floating near the surface, a great danger to little boats as they don't show up on the radar. They also reported huge oil slicks and other pollutant spills sometimes as far as the eye could see.

There was great excitement when one of the most famous sailors pulled in for a stopover in Cape Town and the crew rushed down to interview him. He was obviously going to relax for a couple of days, as by the time they arrived, he was blind drunk and it was difficult to get any sense out of him at all. Conscious that they shouldn't show this hero on national television in such a condition (by now he was totally legless) they managed to prop him against the mast, and coiled a couple of bungee cords round him to hold him upright. Then they took hours of interviews in the hope they could splice his voice into intelligible sentences in the studio.

In the meantime, they would take lots of cutaways, so they would not have to focus on his face too often, a godsend in this case. They did a brilliant job. In the final product, our hero retained his status and no one would ever guess that he was a drivelling wreck with a weak bladder.

Another Johannesburg production company had a contract for making religious programmes that were broadcast every Sunday evening. Again, quite shamelessly - since for quite some time I've been an agnostic or an atheist, I'm never sure which - I pushed my feelings to one side and climbed on the Happy Clappy bandwagon for as long as it took to write the series.

But even I was quite taken back at the opulence of some of the buildings which were a focus for huge congregations each Sunday. They did not pass the collection plate around during the service as I was used to seeing as a child. No, here it was large buckets or wicker baskets large enough to hold a four year old.

Behind the scenes, I was shown their television studio and set up, and my mouth dropped open at the sight of their state of the art equipment. This was stuff that the SABC and most of the other production houses would just die for.

One of the giant supermarkets sponsored a series for 'Good Morning South Africa' on food preparation, using ingredients from their delicatessen range of products. That's what they called their more expensive range in the store areas where they had put black and white tiles on the floor. The shooting budget must have been amazingly large as they flew in top chefs from all over the country to cook these meals in a special kitchen which had been constructed for the occasion. It had real working ovens, and water in the taps, and was the envy of everyone on the crew. We all agreed that if we had a kitchen like this at home, then we too could cook world class meals. In my case, I was lying through my teeth - remember the Mary Baker cake mix disasters?

However the brand new, sparkly kitchen had a downside because it *was* brand new and sparkly. The camera picked up every glitter and shimmer off the shiny handles, cupboards and work surfaces, and spread them into delightful star shapes on the camera lens and monitor. To combat this, professionals use a spray which provides a matt coating over everything, and I'm afraid to tell you, over the food as well if necessary! Frankly, if you attempted to eat anything, you would be wise to phone for the ambulance first.

Not only did they fly in the chefs, they also provided a celebrity anchor lady who would chatter away, asking inane questions as the chef prepared some exotic offering, and then she would taste the finished dish at the end of the programme.

I wonder why no one had thought to ask the anchor lady if she was allergic to any foods, as the first one had quite a few allergies. After a couple of weeks of creative camera work, even the sponsor had to admit that it was perfectly obvious she wasn't even trying to taste the food, so she had to go.

She was replaced in short order, but the next one had to be smartly watched as he was only too keen to sample the results, and we couldn't let him poison himself with non shiny food covered in spray.

Being professionals, the chefs knew the drill and always arrived with a spare dish fully prepared, which was carefully put aside and used only at the end of the show. It bore no relation to the food that was actually cooked in front of the cameras.

Anyone who has ever been on stage will know that theatre lights throw out an enormous amount of heat. It's bad enough in an open auditorium, but in a small kitchen, the temperatures would soar as the day wore on. We were also filming in summer, in Africa, and as you've probably guessed, produce such as fresh fish could go off very quickly indeed. So apart from the frantic spraying over anything shiny, by four o'clock we were all reeling under the stench of rotting fish, or meat, while the smiles on the faces of the celebrity chef and the presenter became fixed and just a little fake as they tried not to gag. Please believe me when I tell you that working in television is not glamorous.

One particularly hot day as we were waiting for our famous cook to arrive, (his plane had been delayed), one of the crew was playing around with a particularly irritating crayfish, which was destined for the pot in an hour or so. He was tickling its feelers with a pencil just to see if he could get it to run about, when much to his horror, the feeler fell off. We all froze in shock. True, we had three crayfish to cover any mishaps, but today's chef was known as a stickler for perfection, and now we had three crayfish, with only five feelers between them.

There was a heated discussion as to how we were going to

try and put the feeler back on, and who was going to do it, while the crayfish scratched around on the table, giving us murderous looks. The antenna was eventually reattached by using a small piece of Prestik or Blu-Tak, and the cameraman threatened with major violence should he show Cuthbert the wounded crayfish, in close up. Our celebrity chef never noticed, and we all breathed a sigh of relief. He had been known to storm off set if everything was not to his liking.

I'm not sure if all chefs have particularly foul tempers, but we certainly met plenty of them on that series and a few more in later years.

As an offshoot of the cookery programmes, which were made in conjunction with a national food magazine, they offered me part-time work proofreading the copy on a weekly basis before it went to print. This was a slightly new field for me, and while I know there are special marks to learn as instructions for the type setters, or the final compositor, or whatever they might be called, I didn't have time to add this knowledge to my list of achievements. But it seems they were happy when I wrote in all the changes clearly by hand on the proofs and handed them back. Even today, I find I proofread menus, timetables, posters, flyers and so on.

I had a brief break when my ex got involved in producing a huge concert in Swaziland to celebrate the King's 21st birthday. The main star was Eric Clapton, with Joan Armatrading and Labi Siffre in supporting roles. Still in Johannesburg, I was liaising with the press and concert providers and got to meet a few more people in the industry, this time on the music side, and one of my favourites was Jonny Clegg.

Apart from some meetings and paperwork, I was not really involved and when it was all over, I could only add 'hot dog salesperson' to my resume as the organizers were each given a free stall in the Swazi village and my ex decided we would make a fortune selling millions of hot dogs over the three day festival.

Unfortunately, our stall was right next door to one selling bunny chows (a half loaf where the dough has been scooped out and then refilled with a meat stew). This proved vastly more popular than the hot dogs. We only sold twelve, and after eating them for a week, in desperation, we passed on the remainder to the local children's hospital. My ex made some remark about them being ill already so week old sausages shouldn't do them much harm.

There were all sorts of ructions behind the scenes before, after and during the concert, but I am not quite comfortable about the libel laws to write about much of it here. I guess a lot of it was hearsay, but many of the stars were difficult to please and their riders were like telephone books.

A rider is a specific set of instructions as to what you must provide for an entertainer. It can be fairly basic, covering information about the kind of hotel, food and drink requirements, set-up in the dressing room, vehicles and drivers to be available and so on. I do know that the management in Swaziland had to send to France for Perrier water at a huge cost, as it was not available in southern Africa at the time, only to find none of it was touched. Another instruction was for 14 lemons cut into quarters for the dressing room, also ignored.

Some riders are just silly - only blue towels, or purple satin sheets or accommodation for numerous friends was to be provided. Something weird must happen to people when they rise to stardom because they seem to lose touch with reality. Does the applause from the crowds persuade them they are more than mere mortals? In fact, if a star does appear friendly and normal, most industry people are quite surprised.

That is one thing I shall never have to worry about. In the

weird and unlikely event of me ever becoming a bestselling author, most of the population wouldn't care or notice. Would you recognize David Baldacci or Wilbur Smith or Barbara Taylor Bradford in the supermarket? No, like me they don't play football and they don't sing. As far as I know they don't.

Not mentioning names, but one of the stars at the Swaziland concert insisted that they stay at the Pigg's Peak Hotel, which was well over a hundred kilometres away from the venue along a very bad mountainous road, and difficult to negotiate after dark.

Another amusing anecdote to come out of the concert came from someone who was there at the time. The King had granted an audience to Eric Clapton and maybe other performers - I'm not sure about that part. The star turned up at the appointed time and had to sit and wait and wait and wait. Eventually the King appeared but I heard he couldn't remember who he was supposed to meet, although he had specifically requested Clapton as the main act for the Birthday Concert. When they came face to face His Majesty did not even recognize Eric.

How much of that story is true I can't say, but I know for certain that the King didn't attend the concert. At the last minute he ordered it to be broadcast directly to the Palace. But that was way beyond the capability of the engineers.

I also know for sure that the Swazi Television Service left one of their cameras fixed to the staging for three days after the concert, as they forgot to remove it and it got very wet. It rained on that first night and one of the early performing band members got electrocuted.

I also remember that I never got to meet Clapton either, remember, I was too busy trying to sell hot dogs.

One of the 32 bands performing at the concert asked my ex if he would manage them, and he agreed. They were quite good, I have to admit that, and they wrote their own music although as a heavy metal band it wasn't quite my kind of music. The outcome was that I got lumbered with running the band since they were in Johannesburg, and I was near Johannesburg while their real manager, my ex, was in Swaziland.

I really didn't need the extra work; I had quite enough to cope with as it was. But it seems that managing meant listening to them all complain about each other for hours each day on the telephone, hiking their demo tape round various possible night club venues, all of which looked decidedly sleazy in the bright light of day, and pitching up to make sure they attended band practice every now and again. It all lasted for maybe eighteen months, and then they went their separate ways.

While I grew more used to the heavy metal music offered by our band, I do prefer light popular music. I like classical music as well - you know, the usual ones such as Mozart, Beethoven, Tchaikovsky and so on, but I was a little unsure about modern classical music. To me it seems a contradiction in terms, because surely to be classical, means it has stood the test of time? For example, Handel's Water Music was the rock music of his era and because it was so good, we still listen to it today.

I was scripting for a series on the Arts programme which was shown very late on a Sunday evening, and I was sent off to get the low down on several up and coming musicians who would be featured each week. To the music world, they may have been up and coming, I would have preferred them to be down and going and preferably out of range.

I can't tell you how many hours I sat through a cacophony of noise as they swayed opposite me with their eyes closed in ecstasy. And being classical, of course, they had written symphonies for exciting instruments such as dustbin lids and steel chair legs, and these lasted for hours and hours and hours. I couldn't wait to escape. I must confess I never even watched the programmes when they were broadcast.

I'll admit that although I know the difference between a bat and a ball, I've never been a sports fan. If I can take part without too much effort, then fine, but I have no desire to watch other people puff and pant and sweat as they go to extreme lengths to be faster or higher than anyone else either. And I'm also not fussed which team wins a cheap silver-plated cup tied with colourful ribbons as a reward for hundreds and hundreds of hours of blood, sweat and tears.

So you might understand my lack of enthusiasm when I was contracted to interview several top sporting personalities who had been chosen by a whisky company as the 'Star of the Month'. For each of the twelve months, one person would be featured and one champion chosen at a massive awards banquet at the end of the year.

With as much enthusiasm as I could gather, I set off on my first interview. My heart sank when the Superstar opened the door. He looked so, well, boring is the only word I can use. We sat in his lounge and sipped coffee as I tried to piece together a brief biography, preferably with a few interesting anecdotes that were not listed on his official publicity blurb. It was like pulling teeth.

"You must have a lot of trophies by now?" I suggested.

"Yes, a few."

"Could I see them?"

With a shrug of his shoulders he got up and I followed him into a nearby room. There were shelves from floor to ceiling against all four walls, on which were dozens and dozens of medals, cups, plaques and framed certificates. I gasped, scribbling down a reminder to shoot these as soon as the cameraman arrived.

"You must be so proud," I murmured in awe.

Another shrug of the shoulders.

"You teach sports at the local school - perhaps we could show that? Can we walk over there so I can get some idea of where and what we can show?"

That was OK, but unfortunately, someone had phoned in a bomb scare, and all the pupils were sitting in long rows on the far side of the playing fields while the bomb squad and their dogs were occupying the school. Maybe it would *not* be a great idea to feature that in the programme.

By this time, the cameraman had arrived and apart from the trophy room, there was very little direction I could give him. I'd now written a list of questions for our Superstar which would give me the information I wanted, but I was worried that his monosyllabic answers would not win him any fans when we put him in front of the camera for his interview.

So, what about a little action? Could we see him in action? As he was a triathlon competitor, could he cycle, or row, or run, so we could show him doing that?

It was like switching on a light bulb, the transformation was so amazing. He gave us a huge smile, came to life and bounded home to get changed and mount his bicycle. The rest of the day's shoot was spent watching our Superstar fly past the camera, left to right and right to left, while I composed suitable words for the voice-over. I'd understood from our conversation in the morning that if Superstar was not actually training or competing he got super-depressed, as I had witnessed earlier.

I thought back to when I'd been told to take out the information that training 'on through the pain barrier' releases the body's natural endorphins, a form of natural morphine that causes a high. But this was a perfect example of just that.

The interview we held to camera as he finally climbed out of his canoe was bright, sparkly and witty, and did we make him look good!

The candidate the following month was a female long distance runner and I was looking forward to meeting her. It nearly didn't happen. Since the producer was busy sorting out a crisis at the time, he pushed a telephone number across the table and told me to ring her agent and set up a day for the interview and shoot.

I duly dialled the number, only to meet a brick wall. Her agent was adamant that she would not appear unless we paid an exorbitant amount of money.

"But this is an honour, and it's for the 'Sports Man or Woman of the Year', chosen live, on national television and each insert featuring all the short-listed people will be shown on television too so people can vote, and again bits of that are shown on the night itself."

Her agent wasn't the slightest bit impressed. No fat fee? No interview, no filming. He hung up on me.

I know in a lot of countries famous people charge a fortune to appear on anything, speak to anyone, or cut a ribbon at the local supermarket, but that culture had not reached South Africa. In those days, people were only too pleased to get the extra publicity. Even if the sponsor was a whisky company they were not throwing their money around, one reason why as the scriptwriter I was on shoot and scripting on the fly next to the cameraman. The award ceremony was going to take almost all the sponsorship money as well as the broadcast of that magic moment awarding the trophy. It goes without saying I was not invited to that, of course.

Plucking up what little courage I could (and I didn't have much to begin with) I tried again, but this time I was not even put through, but firmly rebuffed by the agent's secretary. I went to report my abject failure to the producer, who told me not to worry.

He was back in an hour and handed over a piece of paper with the date and the place where we would record the lady runner.

"How did you do it?" I gasped in admiration.

"Very simple," he replied with a grin.

"Go on then, tell me. I'm amazed."

"It was quite simple really," he replied. "I explained why we wanted to film her, her agent demanded money. I said there was no budget, he said then it was not possible."

"That's exactly what he told me," I said.

"Then I expressed my disappointment, and said that I would have to substitute the second place sports star for this month, but, I promised him I would put a large banner on the screen explaining that his star *was* voted the best, but the budget would not stretch to the interview as her fees were too high, and sadly, we were using the substitute instead."

"And he backed down?" I asked in admiration.

"Instantly! You're filming next Wednesday and that's her address."

Another lesson learned - never dismiss those older and wiser, they know a trick or two! And it was also a reminder of the power of the media.

The runner was charm itself and we spent a great day together. I was tempted to mention that she had a tyrant as a manager, but wisely kept my mouth shut.

I was quite amazed to see that she lived and worked in Sasolburg where they made petrol and oil from coal. By the time the crew car had parked up I was already coughing my lungs up. The air was thick with black dust and it was beyond my comprehension how she could train under such conditions.

The refinery had provided excellent facilities for their employees and the running track was world class, but amid all that air pollution, I could only imagine she had lungs like an elephant. Afterwards, whenever I saw her running on television, I was rooting for her every step of the way - and this from someone who is not the slightest bit interested in sporting events.

13 BANKS, MONEY AND MATHS

In Johannesburg they have a National Film Library that has an enormous selection of educational films they are constantly updating. I was lucky enough to be involved in making some of them, and possibly the most exciting one featured the work being done in Lesotho, where they were building a dam near the source of the Orange River. I honestly cannot remember all the details now, but it was a very complicated project. They had to relocate several villages, giving the inhabitants exactly the same amount of land and buildings as they had occupied previously, plus a couple of years' worth of free seeds to plant.

There were also claims over the ownership of some of the land required to be flooded. A company mining diamonds strongly objected to being ousted, and dug their heels in.

The exciting part was driving to Maseru the capital, to stay in a hotel, all expenses paid. That was a first for me, and I felt very important indeed. I was taken to meet government ministers, all wearing army uniforms, who bombarded me with amazing facts and figures about what was going to happen in the future.

The plan was to go and look at some of the initial earthworks the following day. It was late afternoon by now, and we drove around the capital for a while on our way to the hotel. We were rather surprised that the streets seemed so empty - almost deserted in fact - and then we were stopped at a road block and informed we were out after curfew.

I remember feeling quite alarmed, as up until that moment I

knew little or nothing about this mountain kingdom except for the fact that the people wore blankets and funny straw hats with curly bits on the top.

We were then unceremoniously escorted to our hotel by a couple of army motorbike outriders and once safe in the bar, we learned that after independence from the British in 1966, the Basotho National Party won the first elections. Later they lost to the opposition, and in true African tradition, refused to accept defeat. There was a military coup and King Moshoeshoe II gained power but was later forced into exile when he fell out of favour with the military and his Council of Ministers was purged. And we had walked right into the middle of it.

All thoughts of us roaming the countryside looking at early dam works went out of the window, and I had to make do with several meetings with various engineers in the hotel who drew pictures and explained what they intended to do. In all, I wrote three scripts on the project, which was truly massive, but I never got paid a cent as the whole series of programmes was cancelled and the project was put on hold while the politicians sorted themselves out.

But I couldn't really complain, I'd had a nice trip to Lesotho and a couple of nights in a very nice hotel.

This is one of the downsides of being freelance, but in all the time I was writing, there was only one other occasion when I was refused payment. A company from Port Elizabeth commissioned me to write about the biomes of the Western Cape. Yes, I had no idea what they were either, but in case you're curious, they are particular geographical areas with suitable soil, climate and other conditions which favour unique species of plants.

There is a very important biome around the Cape Town area called the Fynbos Biome which supports the growth of several plants not found naturally anywhere else in the world.

One of these is the protea, the national flower of South Africa and, if I remember correctly, another is the rooibos or red bush plant from which the locals would brew tea, and which has now become popular all over the world.

I thought I did quite a good job, considering the fact that I'm not terribly into plants either, and have been known to kill them off simply by staring at them. I always either drown them or dehydrate them, even though I really do try and care for them and give them a happy home. I've even been known to sing to them on occasion, but that could of course, have contributed to their early demise.

But once I understood what a biome was, it wasn't a difficult script to write and I faxed through my efforts only to receive a return fax telling me I had written a load of rubbish and they were not going to pay me.

I shot another fax straight back to say that if they could tell me where I went wrong, I would happily re-write it to their satisfaction. However, they were not prepared to do that as my efforts were so bad! That was pretty depressing, but it was not possible to visit them as they were in Port Elizabeth several hundred kilometres away.

By chance I had a visit from another writer colleague, full of righteous indignation about this company who were refusing to pay her because she had written such rubbish. My ears perked up. My friend had been in the business a lot longer than me and she just would not write unusable stuff. Yes, it was the same company, and after a little investigation we found two more scriptwriters who had also been told exactly the same thing.

At the time, I was still a member of the South African Scriptwriters Association, as we all were, so we wrote quite a polite letter to the company down in Port Elizabeth expressing our outrage, especially as a friendly spy had informed us that production was well under way! We told the producers quite simply that if we were not paid promptly, then we would inform every scriptwriter in the county, and ban all SASWA members from ever working for them again.

We got paid.

When I think of how everyone in the industry trusted each other, I am amazed we weren't ripped off a lot more, but the teamwork involved and the respect we all had for each other might have something to do with it. Maybe it was just pure luck, but I never heard of any other instances when people were not paid.

Money reminds me of several programmes I made for national banks. One was an hour long, and was aimed at the fledgling entrepreneur. I came up with the concept of a small glass ball that would play any tune as soon as you mentioned the title. This was the product that was going to take the world by storm, but only if our hero did all his marketing correctly, probably by selling his soul to the bank at the same time. The finished programme was to be packaged in a box with several booklets, put out for sale in every branch and advertised in the national press and also on television.

In those days, balancing my chequebook was as financial as it got, and often there were minus signs in front of the totals, but I need not have worried for they provided me with a pet banker who pitched up at the house every morning as we brainstormed ideas, and I wrote the script around them.

I was not involved in the production side on this one as a large Johannesburg film company was awarded the contract. The budget must have been huge as they hired in well-known actors to play the parts; and they used quite extensive top-end graphics to represent the cartoon characters which popped up at opportune moments. They gave this rather witless inventor lots of good advice, from the bank's point of view of course. I noticed that our hero was up to his eyes in debt, having put up his house, wife, coin collection and hideously expensive goldfish as collateral to the bank, in return for the start up capital. Poor devil, he had no idea what might be in store for him in the future if the interest rates went up.

I had been seduced by the glamour of working in television, but it was a much, much harder medium to work in. The upside was that a lot more people were involved and this often sparked ideas for writing. Not that I had the luxury of suffering from 'writer's block'. When you have broadcast deadlines to meet, you just can't afford to have that. The ideas for the drama stories had to come from somewhere, and even though I explained to the family that walking round the pool really was work, I'm sure they didn't believe me. After three years or so, it was getting more difficult to pull imaginary rabbits out of the hat, and it was something of a relief to be able to script on factual things and report on subjects that did not require a storyline.

I still had ideas such as the programme on potato chips, which I wrote from the point of view of an excellently grown tuber on a special farm. He was just so thrilled to have been chosen to be one of their potato chips. Pretty stupid really. If only he'd known he was going to be scrubbed raw and then thrown into a vat of boiling oil, that would have wiped the smile off his face.

Years later I saw a commercial on television with exactly the same theme - dancing potatoes which were destined for the chip packet. There are probably few, really different ideas left after all.

The experiences I had on the fringes of the corporate world opened my eyes. As I had previously lived in the classroom for most of my life, I had not been exposed to the world of manufacturing, and I found it a complete revelation.

I was quite convinced that I could never get almost orgasmic over a packet of chips, or worry a new cream cake might not be a financial success. I would never be enthralled by the uses of aluminium, panic about the number of pills people poured down their throats, or fret that an advertising campaign to boost sales of photographic film, or lounge suites, or a low fat spread, might not reach targets.

But during my research, I met all kinds of people who were totally committed to their products and I had to admire them.

If I was honest, I too was passionate about my work, to entertain and inform. I know this sounds horribly immodest, but I wanted to improve lives, especially among those with less education and those who did not start out very high on the ladder of success. Even in later years when I worked in an advertising agency for a short time (I think I freelanced for all of three weeks), my heart wasn't in it. I didn't care a damn if people bought Palmolive, or Pears or Sunlight soap, I didn't feel it was important. For me, helping people to live happier and healthier lives was.

On one bizarre occasion I was called in to write the newspaper copy for Checkers, a large chain of supermarkets in South Africa.

"The budget was announced on the radio this afternoon," they said.

Yes, I knew that, I had listened carefully to find out how much extra tax they were going to put on booze and fags. I wasn't feeling too happy with the increases either.

"We want to write a letter to thank the Minister for an excellent budget," they explained further.

I did a double take. Thank the Minister? In England the moment the red budget box is opened and the contents revealed, everyone climbs on the bandwagon snarling and spitting, and there is always condemnation and criticism. You can't please all of the people all of the time and you are

165

bound to upset some. The opposition in particular have a field day, even if those measures are the very same ones they would have introduced themselves.

I think my smarmy, sucking up letter to the Finance Minister, appearing as a full page spread in every newspaper the following day was perhaps the most nauseating piece I have ever produced. Thankfully, being an advertisement, it did not have my name on it.

Some person at the SABC must have passed on the word that I was a real teacher in my former life, because I was approached by a lady who had worked for both the SABC and a national newspaper. She wanted me to write for a maths series to be broadcast on television. Maths! I gasped. She had to be joking - I have never passed a maths exam in my life, a fact I'd been successfully hiding for decades. Silly little numbers scared me witless. I could just about calculate how much material I needed for curtains, and how to cost out the weekly food shop, but anything more than that and I was stumped.

We all filed into a boardroom in the SABC and I eyed up the other writers. They looked intelligent and smart and although I had once again taken my jeans off for the occasion (at home I must hastily add), I felt less than confident.

The first priority was to share out the programmes as they would feature algebra, geometry and arithmetic.

Please don't give me geometry, I prayed. I know nothing about geometry, and algebra would be a nightmare too. The best option must be the arithmetic, I'll opt for that.

Too late! While I sat there panicking, the other two jumped in at the speed of light, and I came to just in time to hear the producer say "And that leaves Lucinda for the geometry programmes."

My heart sank. I remembered those hours in the classroom

sweating buckets hoping the teacher wouldn't ask me a question. I could never grasp that if two sides of a triangle were a certain length then the other side must be.... and so on.

"Maths is such an exciting subject, so I know we can make these programmes interesting," continued the producer, who I later learned had been a maths teacher in a former life. "So, I know you are going to make them really fascinating and fun."

Just who was she kidding? Then she dropped another bombshell. "Here are the contact numbers for the professors. Yours is at the University in Pretoria, Lucinda. He will be your subject specialist, so show him your list of topics and he will give you all the help you need."

I doubt any professor would have enough time to help me if we had to start with the nine times table, I thought, as I drove home in a panic. I realized that this time in my enthusiasm, I had bitten off more than I could chew. I couldn't decide if it was only my greed which had overcome my common sense, or a fear of turning down a promised pay cheque, or the drive to pay the bills that came flooding in on a daily basis.

Feeling quite terrified, a couple of days later I drove to Pretoria and onto the campus of Tukkies University. This is one of the most prestigious halls of learning and for the most part operates in Afrikaans. I could only hope that the professor who was going to be my subject specialist spoke good English. I didn't need matters to get any worse.

When I eventually found his office, I was amazed that in such a smart compound they had allocated this important man a room the size of a rabbit hutch. I was also slightly alarmed to see that he was wearing a pair of mismatched socks. Surely that only happened in the movies, didn't it?

After the handshakes and the orders for coffee, we got down to business as I handed him the list of geometry topics for the series. He read them and nodded, so at least one of us understood what they were. I'd been thinking about this on the drive over, and decided that the child actors in the series should build something and use geometry in the construction. My first idea was to have a pregnant, stray dog the children had rescued from a near certain death, so obviously they needed to build her a kennel, didn't they?

As I explained this to the professor, he looked more than a little alarmed. I then went on to describe other possible scenarios I thought might match some of the other content to do with angles and shapes and so on. But there was one theorem which was bothering me. Firstly, I barely understood it, and secondly I hadn't a clue what you would do with it practically in real life. So cheerfully I asked the professor how we could demonstrate this.

"I don't know," he replied.

"Um, yes, but how would you apply it in real life?"

"No idea."

"But it's on the syllabus?"

"Yes."

"And if we are asking children to learn how to prove this theorem, there must be a reason, surely?"

"Yes."

"Uh, so why.....? I mean, how can they use it later on?"

"I can't think of anything really."

"So, if it's not a daft question, why is it on the syllabus if it appears to be useless?"

"Um, well..." he paused for a very long think. "It teaches discipline in thinking," he replied. "Yes, it teaches them disciplined thinking."

Great, I thought. How was I going to weave a story around that? Not that the professor thought much of my story ideas at all. He was expecting a 'chalk and talk' explanation to the camera by someone such as himself, and I think he was a bit miffed that he was not going to be starring in the series. I briefly wondered what wardrobe would say about his mismatched socks.

I tried to perk up his enthusiasm for a fun, entertaining way to get the children on board that geometry was exciting and useful and a good thing to know. It was not a good start. While I was trying to get the Prof on board, I was also trying to fool myself into believing the same thing.

Eventually, after several trips backwards and forwards with one version of the script after another, I had built the dog kennel, and a host of other absolutely necessary things, except for the one on the syllabus for 'disciplined thinking'. I decided to make this particular theorem fit the bill by making it a group school project. I sent the children to the airport to discover how far off the ground the wing of a jumbo jet was, I was really stretching matters here. I'm not even sure how closely related the theorem was to what they were about to find out, but by now I was quite desperate.

My subject specialist appeared to have lost interest and was never available to help, and even by sneaking into all the newsagents and bookshops, I could find no easy workbooks on the topic of theorems which might help me out. I ploughed ahead regardless on that final script and the nice producer lady never batted an eyelid.

I was not involved in the production side of the series at all, which was probably just as well. I heard on the grapevine that the production team were about to put out a hit on a writer named Lucinda E Clarke, who had given them the problem of finding a pregnant dog who would behave in the studio, professionally trained ones were way out of budget. Then to make matters worse, she had sent them all off to Johannesburg Airport for the day and they were expected to get crystal clear sound amid all the landings and take offs, plus getting permission to go airside with a bunch of unruly children.

I thought it wise to keep a low profile for a couple of weeks, but remembered with a shudder that initially in my first script outline, I had included the dog in the trip to the airport too.

Part of the maths series had been farmed out to Cape Town and Durban, the two other major cities in South Africa. There had been complaints that Johannesburg, which is not strictly the capital (that is Pretoria, or Tshwane as it is called these days) was taking the lion's share of the production and the scriptwriting work.

It's one of those anomalies that everyone thinks of Johannesburg as the capital, although it is certainly the centre for finance and industry. In fact even Pretoria is not a stand-alone capital - it shares that place with Cape Town as the parliament hops from one to the other on a half yearly basis. How's that for inefficiency?

I can't remember now what the difficulties were in Durban over the maths series, but much to my amazement the producer decided to fly me down there to sort out the problems. They must have been logistical and not mathematical surely? Either that or my acting had improved considerably and the producer was convinced I knew what I was talking about.

This time, I flew down on a commercial flight, was met at Durban Airport by an SABC employee, and driven to the broadcast offices on Old Fort Road. He drove around the back of the building and into the car park, hopped out, pointed to a car and threw me a bunch of keys.

This was a bit of a shock as the meeting was at the University of Durban Westville and I had no idea how to get there. I managed to call out to him just before he disappeared from view.

"Take the N3 out of Durban inland and just as you get to Westville. You will see it on your right hand side, you can't miss it."

Dubiously I got into the car and tentatively drove off. You know what it's like getting into a car you've not driven before, all the knobs, buttons and levers are all in the wrong places. I had no idea what was what, as I turned on the windscreen wipers to indicate I was turning left.

The meeting went off satisfactorily and I managed to console the distraught scriptwriter, who was totally at odds with her subject specialist. Although I did not go so far as to admit I'd never passed a maths exam in my life, I got them working together again, and mapped out her remaining three episodes.

It was time to go home to the Reef, which refers to the area covering Johannesburg, Pretoria and the gold mining regions around what is now referred to as Gauteng. I don't think it matters which country you live in, there is always a certain prestige about residing in the capital city. It gives you status, and a certain air of competence. If you can survive in the competitive world of the capital, you are perceived to have 'made it'.

So it was with an air of assurance that I went back outside to the car park and prepared to drive back to the SABC, drop off the car and be driven to the airport. As I prepared to leave, I discovered that I did not know how to go backwards. *I* could go backwards - it was the car I couldn't reverse. I gazed at the knob on the gear lever, but that was completely smooth and shiny and didn't give me a clue as to which way I should waggle it. I tried the gear stick in every conceivable position, but every time I lifted my foot off the clutch, I moved ever further forward, until at last, the bumper was right up against the kerb. I was tempted for a moment to rev the engine and mount the kerb, but on the other side of the narrow pavement, were well tended flower beds, bordering a beautifully kept, green lawn beyond. I was stuck, and there was no one in sight.

I hopped out and went to ask for help at the reception desk, but it was deserted. I walked down a couple of the passageways desperately looking for someone to ask, but you'd think that the rest of humanity had evaporated in a passing time machine.

I went back to the car and considered trying to put it into neutral and push it backwards, but what if it went out of control and crashed into another car? I didn't feel quite so confident now, and I kept glancing at my watch, time was galloping on and I had a plane to catch. If I missed it, I didn't have enough money for another ticket, and they were not going to accept my maxed out credit card either.

Eventually I saw a figure emerge from the building, and I raced across the car park, accosted him and blurted out my problem. Of course he thought it extremely funny, and came and showed me how to wrap my fingers round the gear stick and pull up the rubber collar that would allow the car to drop into reverse gear.

What a stupid piece of obviously male engineering, I thought, as I raced back down the hill into Durban. What idiot designed a gear stick that worked like that?

Which reminds me of another time I hired a car at the airport, and they handed me the keys to one without a gear stick at all! I had specifically asked for a manual, as although we had owned automatic cars in the past, I prefer to feel more in control - changing down to race past a truck, for example. As I sat in the driving seat trying to puzzle out the various levers, bells and whistles in this shiny brand-new car, which I am convinced had more indicators, screens and flashing lights than the cockpit in the average jumbo jet; I realized that I would not be able to change gear. I rushed back into their office and complained.

"Didn't you see the button on the floor?" they asked.

"Button? What button?"

"You press it when you want to change gear."

"No thanks, when I want to change gear I want to use a lever like I've always done. Can you please give me another car, and a proper one this time."

I may be a Luddite, but while I'm prepared to move with the times, I have my limits and this does not include absent gear sticks.

My humble maths script offerings may not have been as accurate as the others in the series but they were a lot more fun, and I was commissioned for another series. This time it was interviewing characters from the English literature books that were the set pieces on the syllabus for Matriculation, and end of year exams. I had a great time re-reading Shakespeare, Dickens and a whole range of books by African novelists I'd never heard of. While I hated the classics in school because they were inflicted on me, now I could appreciate them and see the merits they had as great works of literary art.

But when I switched on the TV one day, I was horrified to see that Julius Caesar was wearing short, white wellington boots! I'll never forgive wardrobe - what were they thinking? As I watched the broadcast, I saw that his toga was snowy white, his haircut was precise, the laurel leaves surrounding his head looked magnificent, and then you caught sight of his white patent boots shining under the studio lights!

Maybe it was the crew's revenge for the pregnant Labrador they had running around the studio a couple of months ago? Or maybe they had not enjoyed their day at the airport?

I still have a couple of these programmes on tape I recorded off the television, but they were the last to be recorded in a local production studio. In future, all programmes commissioned for broadcast were to be produced in the SABC studios, which was another little trick the broadcasting bully came up with. Yes, they would commission series, but you had to use all their facilities, for which they would charge you.

So as the producer walked in ready to rehearse, they were waiting with a bill for studio time, wardrobe, make up, the hire of one or more cameras, sound, lights and so on, the cost of the set, and of course, the in-house SABC operators as well.

All that was left at the end of the day for the producer to put in the bank was the fees she had allocated for herself, out of which she was paying the scriptwriter and the cast. Everyone was furious about this situation, but there was nothing anyone could do. In those days the SABC was not only run by the government, and was its mouthpiece, it had little or no competition. A second channel called M-Net had recently started up, but the viewership was quite small as it was a subscription service, and you had to buy a decoder. The majority of their airtime showed American movies in the early days and they were not yet commissioning many local productions.

Of course there was a lot of creative paperwork going on, with wildly inflated prices for sourcing anything the SABC could not provide, such as research, and transport costs, and any other rabbit they could pull out of the hat. But the bottom line was the SABC were simply hiring in producers as they had a dearth of personnel in that department, and the rest of the industry could take it or leave it.

The Schools Television programmes we had been working on were not high budget and they were more hassle than they were worth, so sadly for me, my nice lady producer finally had enough and she decided to return to Ireland and take early retirement. Another door closed.

14 GOODBYE JOHANNESBURG

There was one big plus about working in the industry at that time. I was lucky to be working in television and video when South Africa had few, if any, restrictions. We were pretty much free to take the cameras out and about and accost people on the street, or in the workplace or homes if we asked politely. The only places we tried to avoid were the interiors of restaurants, especially the dark, candle lit ones.

Because of the problems with lighting?

No.

Because we might get in the way of the waiters?

No.

Because we couldn't set up a broadcast camera in a confined space where the tables were close together?

No.

Because the candles might set light to the camera gear?

No.

So why?

The dangers of recording people in the background who were not dining with the people they were supposed to be dining with! One crew in Johannesburg accidently caught a boss and his secretary dining in a most intimate manner when he was supposed to be overseas or at a business conference elsewhere. When it aired on television, and his wife or one of her friends happened to see it, all hell broke loose. It didn't take long for every restaurant owner in the country to ban crews and cameras. We were very bad for business.

This was a terrible nuisance, for if we needed a dining scene, we had to hire in extras, and they were expensive, and

175

if the location was small and intimate they quickly got underfoot. You have no idea how often people - especially the elderly, retired people who hired themselves out for a day, (they were decidedly cheaper than the younger ones), needed the restrooms. So it was up and down, up and down, up and down. Have you ever noticed how distracting it can be when you are trying to concentrate on the two main actors closest to the camera if the people behind them are bouncing about like kangaroos?

These days I feel very guilty, as on shoot at the end of a long, hot and tiring day, I would get quite irate with some of the extras. Now I am elderly myself, I have the same problems. How our behaviour in youth comes back to haunt us. I wish I'd had more understanding.

For many of our extras, it seemed a glamorous way to earn an extra few Rand, but it can be both tiring and deadly dull. They might be asked to stand for ages, pretending to have fake conversations with other 'extra' people they don't know, or walk backwards and forwards behind the lead characters who might fluff their lines time and time again. If they got to sit down in a restaurant for example, after three hours of bum-numbing chairs, no food and only cold tea to drink, sometimes they didn't turn up the next day, which threw your continuity out of the window.

Continuity was always the pit waiting to engulf you if you were not on your toes. I had my own nemesis (which I describe in my next book), but on larger budget programmes you could afford to have a professional who watched every move on a monitor and recorded every wriggle and wiggle. Even in Hollywood they make mistakes, and some bright sparks started to make television programmes out of these, featuring errors that some sharp-eyed viewer has noticed, and they've become very popular.

I remember one large series I worked on for a major

pharmaceutical company in England which was training detail men. I'd never heard of the term, but apparently they're the guys who trawl around doctors' surgeries and pharmacies, peddling certain drugs for the medical company which employs them.

They'd built two sets in the large conference room of a downtown Johannesburg hotel, which was very handy, as we all climbed on the bandwagon and ordered copious cups of coffee from morning until night. We had those waiters running up and down stairs, and in and out of the lifts, with tray after tray after tray of the stuff.

One set showed a very realistic pharmacy counter and we had extras hovering around in the background pretending to buy, which is quite tiring if you pick up, peer at and then put down empty pill boxes for a couple of hours at a time. The continuity lady we had on that shoot was determined not to let anything by her and she would shout "Cut" at every opportunity. Eventually the director got the hell in with her, as she ran the tape back on the monitor and pointed out a discrepancy which was only apparent to her and her alone.

As if by magic, on the last day of the week-long shoot, the hotel had had enough, and the free coffee supply dried up. There was not a waiter in sight, and strangely, they seemed to have disconnected the phones from the conference centre to the rest of the hotel. As a result, rather odd I thought at the time, not a single, solitary continuity problem was noted that day and we packed up in record time.

I also worked on a series for Schools Television called 'Science Club'. I have to admit that my grasp of scientific subjects is only fractionally better than my maths, remember the number of times I had to be dragged out of science class? I just don't have that sort of brain.

This time there was a huge crowd of scriptwriters and I was

only allocated about six episodes, and although I needed the money, I was rather grateful that I would not have to labour over too many of them. I was not involved in the production, but as it was for a really nice lady producer who had been a writer herself, I was invited to the wrap party. I felt a little out of place as I knew no one there, and of course every other person knew everyone else, they had been practically living together for the previous six weeks. They had no idea who the strange middle-aged lady standing in the corner talking to the pot plant was. It wasn't the most scintillating event I have attended, but it was a free meal.

I had no idea that at the end of a series everyone gathered to eat, drink and chat about how the production had gone. Before, I had either written at home in solitary isolation, or worked on the production side in-house, and we certainly didn't have time to party with a deadline to meet every week. So a wrap party was a novelty to me. It still is. As I would tell my first year fledgling scriptwriters in Durban Technikon many years later, if you wanted to be famous, forget being a scriptwriter. Most people don't care who wrote, shot, lit or provided the props to a programme however good it was. Their eyes are on the main actors, who to be quite honest are only repeating the lines, reacting and moving in various directions according to the script, which is someone else's work, your script, if you work hard enough over the next three years.

Since the unions in America have insisted that everyone, right down to the third cameraman's boyfriend, is mentioned in the credits, these can now roll up the screen for hours and hours, or at such a speed they are quite impossible to read.

In the meantime, the audience is outside on the pavement lighting up a cigarette, or, if at home, they are in the bathroom, or putting the kettle on and the cat out. No one cares.

"If you want to be famous and well-known," I would say, "then leave now and make for the drama department."

In all my years of production work, the crew knew better than to catch me on camera. The camera hates me, and even when I was interviewing in the streets, they were only allowed to show the microphone and my wrist, possibly the most photogenic part of my anatomy.

Now I have never earned my living on the streets, but I have earned pennies standing on the pavement accosting passers-by to say a few words to the camera. In the industry it is known as *vox populi,* (vox pops) or 'voice of the people' in Latin, and maybe it is easier in Europe or America, but in South Africa it was torture.

I waited as people approached and I would smile and try to get out the opening phrase before they swept past me. Some of them would take one look and cross to the other side of the road, while others would race by after giving me a dirty look.

As a result I always captured those kind folk with very few brain cells who didn't understand the question, and were quite incapable of giving me a competent reply.

On the odd occasion when I was really desperate, I did the unmentionable and roped in friends and backroom production staff to give me any reasonable answer. The problem with that was, I could only use them once, or it totally gave the game away!

Although apartheid in South Africa has a terrible name around the world, and the whites have been branded as the bad guys, there were an incredible number of people actively working to help uplift and further educate other races. One of these was a man whose name I've sadly forgotten, who used part of his yearly company profits to sponsor an annual careers road show called 'Future Finders'. The initiative was also supported by the Small Business Development

Corporation, government departments and a range of NGO's - non-governmental organizations.

The caravan train would arrive in towns and cities, packed with all kinds of information about finding jobs for both qualified and unqualified youngsters. There was a tie in with SABC television and radio programmes with interviews, real life stories and give-aways to attract the crowds. The idea was to get the youth happily and gainfully employed, open up the world of possible work, and maybe even introduce careers they didn't know existed.

Part of the package included a magazine costing 2 Rand, (about 25 cents), fostering the idea anything given for free was not appreciated. I can't remember now how I got involved, but before I realized it, I was responsible for gathering the content and getting the whole thing printed.

This was a new field for me and I was rather out of my depth. I had written for several magazines but I had never put one together before. It was very gratifying that the man driving the whole campaign thought I was capable of producing this masterpiece, but I suspect he mentally lumped the media world of videos and printed matter together as one, which is certainly not the case.

As you will have realized by now, I will do almost anything for money so I accepted the job before I even thought how I was going to find the material. I asked around, but no one was willing to help, they were all too busy, and I didn't have a team of people allocated to take on part of the project.

I was given a spare office in the corporate building, a Macintosh computer I didn't know how to use, and instructions to go to the graphic designer when I had all the copy ready for him to paginate.

It wasn't too difficult to put together information on careers such as hotel management, or teaching, as they had fixed training requirements, and I went to interview Clive Rice the international cricketer, who gave me advice on how to succeed in sport. It was the more informal work that was more of a problem.

I rifled through the scripts I had written quite some time ago for SABC radio on how to earn a living, and that became an article on twelve great ways to make money. But I still needed real life stories to include. I had a brainwave. Perhaps I could include Shadrack Khopotse, our pool pump cover man and I arranged to go and see him.

I found him in his own office, smartly dressed in a suit and tie. He was now employing over sixty people and had brought his two sons into the business. Together they manufactured fibreglass chairs, boxes, canoes, baths and covers for conveyor belts and it was great to see him doing so well. While I was trying to get lots of tips from him to write about, he only had one. "Hard work, hard work, that is what it is about. No success without hard work," he repeated over and over again. I dutifully wrote it down, reminding myself that to mention all this hard work once in the article would be sufficient.

Luckily someone else sent in a contribution about another small successful screen printing company, but the deadline was looming and I had no informal success stories to write about. In desperation, I wrote them myself. It wasn't strictly ethical I guess, but we had to include some less ambitious ways of earning a living that appeared to be true. I asked the in-house photographer to set up a shoe shine boy and bring me the photograph. I'm not sure he quite got the point, as I've yet to meet a shoe shine boy wearing a shirt and tie, but he did have a happy smile.

I didn't have to write the Career Agony Aunt article, nor make up the crossword, thank goodness, but I was told to write the horoscopes. I never realized how tricky it is to write twelve short pieces containing some hope, some warnings and lots of encouragement.

Years later, a friend of mine who worked on a large provincial paper was designated to write the horoscopes for two weeks while the psychic lady was on holiday - apparently she couldn't see that far into the future. He said he really enjoyed it, as he was going through a nasty divorce at the time, and wrote dire warnings and doom and gloom every day for his soon to be ex-wife's star sign.

I mentioned there was a tie-in from 'Future Finders' with the television, and one channel was devoted for a whole weekend with wall to wall programmes, inserts, interviews and panel discussions all about careers. It was an amazing initiative, mostly hosted by young people themselves from all walks of life.

A spin off from the booklet I wrote for the bush mothers at Medunsa was the catalyst for an approach from my editor at Heinemann to ask me to write an educational book for the Standard 4 syllabus in schools. It was eventually published by MacMillan as my editor moved over to them. Writing the book wasn't too difficult. I combed the Children's Encyclopaedia which had been the best things I had ever purchased, thanks to the weaselly, pimply youth with the stringy hair. It all went well until they asked me to illustrate it. I can't even draw a smiley face! I explained this to them hoping it would get me off the hook, but no such luck. They did explain that my drawings wouldn't actually be used in the final publication, but I had to indicate to the illustrator what I wanted him or her to draw.

I honestly did my best, but I was told that it took the artist a long time to begin work as he was laughing so much.

I had read about royalties, and I hoped this might be a financial breakthrough, but no such luck. MacMillan had given me a sizeable chunk in the way of an advance, allowing me to work on it full time for several weeks and not chase other work. By the time this was paid back, and the publishers, printers and who knows who else, had taken their cut, my final royalties came to £4.10! Is it any wonder I've decided to go the Indie self-publishing route now I'm writing books again?

Mind you, I don't think it sold all that well. Although it was accepted onto the prescribed book list with the South African Education Department, it didn't help to pay the bills.

My editor asked me to represent them at a 'Writing Books for Children' course to be held for a week in Johannesburg. It was great fun and for the first time I met and chatted to other writers and compared notes. Writers seldom got to meet each other in those days, long before Facebook and Twitter and so on. Many never got involved in the production side at all, and as this was a course for book writing, I was the only one there who worked in a different media format.

It was also the first time I met Gcina Mhlope, who is one of South Africa's renowned actresses and story tellers. She kept us all amused during the lunch breaks with her stories of African folklore and I promised myself that one day, if there was ever an opportunity, I would ask for her to take a part in something I had written.

I didn't know it at the time, but Gcina could tell her stories in English, Afrikaans, Zulu and Xhosa. She has performed all over Europe and America and is very popular in South Africa.

I remember one interesting fact she told us, and it still puzzles me today. In English, and I guess a lot of other languages as well, a story has a beginning, a middle and an end. We probably all remember that being drummed into us at school. Traditional African stories are different, they simply go on and on and on, in what Gcina described as the washing-line effect. You put up the line and then you hang all the stories on it. I wasn't quite sure what she meant, and the only explanation I can think of, is that sitting outside a rural African hut, in the long warm evenings, perhaps the story teller moved from one story to the next, never wrapping one up completely, but branching off as he or she thought of another one.

Later, when I was lecturing in scriptwriting, I often noticed that many of the students did not present a beginning, middle and end to the story and you were often left high and dry, just like that washing-line.

It was several years later, when we met up again, and I'm proud to say she agreed to appear in one of my programmes.

Back at the SABC, I was asked to write the links for a programme called Eduspectrum, which was going to be shot all over the country, using local school children as the presenters in each location. I needed to research each town to find out what was interesting and extraordinary about each one.

Today that would be so easy with the Internet, and it would only take a couple of minutes, but in the late 1980s it took me hours reading the faithful encyclopaedias and combing through travel guides in the library. With the larger towns, this was not too big a problem, but when they chose tiny 'dorps,' the Afrikaans name for a one-horse sort of town, this was a big challenge. For example, I only found out at the very last moment that Ficksburg is well-known for its cherries. Now how on earth was I supposed to know that? The instant I knew this, out went the blurb about it being near the Lesotho border, and in went the cherries.

We take the Internet so much for granted now and it saves us hours and hours of our time. I thought that I had a modern, up to date fully equipped office, with a computer, photocopier and fax facilities which in those days used thermal paper, which fades over time. So despite all my investment, every week I had to drive the forty kilometres into Auckland Park to deliver the hard copy scripts.

I cannot remember all the programmes I wrote and helped produce, and I can't even search for them, since the early ones were archived onto floppy disks, and then later onto the smaller stiffy disks and nowadays they are stored on CDs and DVDs. Each time I upgraded my technology, there never seemed to be enough time to transfer it back onto the computer and save it in the new format.

I've lost all my ideas accepted by MacMillan in Oxford for the series of children's books I didn't have time to write, and do you think I can remember any of them? Which reminds me, I must type faster, as my memory is failing me by the day!

Due to the long hours and the pressure of coping with an overload of work, I suffered burn out twice in those years, taking to bed for most of the long Christmas break that's also the summer holidays in South Africa.

We often went down to stay with our friends who had moved from Pretoria to a little place west of Durban. The rest of the family spent days on the beach and the remaining time in the shops.

I had been working nonstop for years and I had become so exhausted that eventually I agreed to leave and go live on the boat we had partly bought and which was floating in Durban Harbour. How and why all this came about I have covered in my first memoir, so I won't repeat it here, but the idea was for me to move down with the children and while they were at school, I would sit happily in the Yacht Club and begin my new career as a novelist.

It wasn't to be.

15 HELLO DURBAN

The first housekeeping cheque bounced and I was once again on the hunt for work. I phoned the SABC and told them I was available after all, and they immediately gave me a commission to visit a local Technical School outside Durban, research it and write a half-hour programme on their courses and facilities.

I jumped in the car the following day, armed with a map and was a little alarmed as I saw the college was right in the middle of a large township. I'd been in many black townships before, but it was always with other crew members, usually black Africans. This time I was going in on my own. Visions of being hijacked raced through my mind, and the hairs on the back of my neck were standing on end, especially when I realized that I'd taken the wrong turning. It felt like hundreds of pairs of eyes were weighing me up, and there was not another white face in sight. It wasn't unheard of for cars to be stopped, and the drivers relieved violently of their valuables.

I drove round and round; the map didn't seem to be too accurate and it was only by chance that I noticed a likely looking group of buildings with lots of young adults hanging around outside. I drove in, confirmed with one of the students I had reached the right place, and they directed me to the administration block.

Everyone was very friendly, eager to take part in the programme and happy to show what the college had to offer and I was taken on a conducted tour of the facilities. While walking around with one of the lecturers and a couple of students, I was puzzled by a statue that had obviously been vandalized. They noticed my interest and explained that it had been put up in honour of Chief Buthelezi, head of the mainly Zulu Inkatha Freedom Party, but that some of the students who were supporters of the African National Congress had destroyed it.

I became aware that all was not as peaceful as it seemed, and the campus was split into opposing factions and these conflicts are seldom settled amicably in Africa. The drive back to Durban was an uncomfortable one, and I think I broke the speed limit once or twice.

My old friends from the Radio Department also came to my rescue. One of the producers hopped on a plane, flew down and took me to lunch at the Royal Hotel while we discussed the outline of another series. This was way better than an SABC boardroom with their never changing fare of weak coffee and stale nibbles.

I bought an extension lead and set up the rather large laptop I'd acquired, and worked in the Yacht Club every day. As I phoned for the courier I breathed a sigh of relief that I would finally have money coming in.

I didn't make as large a profit as I might have done a few weeks before. To validate me sitting in the Royal Natal Yacht Club all day I felt compelled to purchase a nonstop supply of coffee and a daily lunch. Also as I got to know more people, there were constant interruptions as they would meander over for a chat. They seemed a bit puzzled that a writer would be sitting writing in a public place, when surely it was a private, solitary occupation?

Since our old neighbours from the Reef lived several kilometres out of Durban, the only other contact I had was a production company I'd spoken to once before. I went to visit them, and after showing me numerous videos they'd made of wild birds, they invited me to the next meeting of the Durban branch of the National Television and Video Association. I noted the date and the place and arranged to meet them there. They promised to introduce me to other people in the same industry and I was just praying that someone just might have work for me.

The following week I took the lift to the eleventh floor of one of the tallest buildings in Durban, and tentatively peered round the corner of the open door to see a large crowd of people. It seemed the whole of the video industry was attending, except for the only people I knew. I was quite terrified, but decided to have one drink and beat a hasty retreat.

Outside of work, I was not used to attending social functions on my own, but I needn't have worried. I got chatting to a guy who told me he was a cameraman for the Durban City Council in-house video unit. I learned that Durban was one of only two city councils in the world, along with Westminster in London, which had a healthy bank balance, so they could afford to employ two full-time people to make educational and promotional programmes for the city. He introduced me to the guy he worked with and they wanted to know what I was doing in Durban.

"You've worked in Johannesburg?"

"Yes."

"You wrote scripts?"

"Yes."

"Would you like to come in and have a look at how we work?"

"Yes, I would love to."

"We'll see you tomorrow at about ten."

They never mentioned anything about work, but at least it was a start.

The next morning I walked into their offices at ten, and walked out again two hours later with a commission to write two programmes under very favourable terms.

I'll never forget that first brief. It was on the theme 'Why Pay for Water?' The Durban City Council was installing potable water into the informal settlements at a small cost to each householder, but although the homeowners wanted a clean water supply right outside their houses, they were not prepared to pay anything at all for it. My job was to convince them that giving it away for free was not financially viable.

All the local people could plainly see that fresh, clean water fell free from the skies as a gift from God, and being asked to pay for it, was obviously a conspiracy by the white man to keep them poor and downtrodden. It was a matter of changing mindsets, and that is not an easy thing to do.

I decided the only way to persuade them was to show that having clean water improved their health, it gave them status in the community, and how someone had to pay all the workers who installed and provided the fresh water supply.

They liked the script, which I wrote at my usual breakneck speed and after they had read it through, they asked me if I would like to go on shoot and act as Production Secretary and see it all come together. Yes, I would! I danced back to the boat.

Now, I've never believed that I am any great shakes at being a brilliant writer, my scribbling will never get on the prescribed book list for exams nor go down in history as great literature. Any success I had I put down to those days being trained to teach children, and learning to break down information into bite sized chunks - presenting it in several different ways if necessary until most, if not all the children understood.

When it came to writing scripts, I found it very easy, and I am quite ashamed to admit that I scribbled them at an indecent speed, sometimes in a matter of minutes. I have been known to sit on a finished piece for a couple of days as I did not want the client to know how quickly I had worked; they might just think they were paying me too much!

I had also been taught about attention spans, and how even adults cannot concentrate for all that long before wandering thoughts pop up, like:

"Did I turn the gas off before I came out?" or "Where have I put the parking ticket?"

So the average length of a video aimed at the township residents should not last longer than fifteen or twenty minutes at the most, even if it was dramatized.

A subject such as 'Why Pay for Water?' had a lot of aspects - paying the men who worked in the Water Department, raising awareness of using clean water with the benefits to health, thus saving medical expenses, growing your own vegetables if you can irrigate them, and so on. I'm sure you get the drift.

Being a little crafty, I had suggested to the producers that this topic needed two programmes, and they had agreed. This was a win-win situation - better programmes, and more money for me, what could be nicer than that?

The first programme was to show the health benefits and needed to be shot in a squatter camp, so they chose a location quite close to the city centre. I was relieved to see that we had a Council manager with us and he brought one of the black workers with him as well. I'd never gone into such an area with an all white crew, you need at least one person who can speak the local language.

We had a crew of four - Brian and Carl from the video unit, Shezi who they had recently poached from another production house, and me.

We filmed for a week in the squatter camp where we had permission to use a house while the family was out at work. As often happens, we attracted a large and curious crowd who thought we were all quite mad, as the Council workers slowly converted one bog standard packing case shack into a home worthy of the modern family who had signed up for a new tank and fresh water supply.

First they painted the house a delicate shade of blue, but only on the two sides the camera would show. Then more Council workers cleared the ground around the house, putting in a row of flowers from the municipal nurseries, edged with ornamental stones. The larger piece of land in front of the shack was raked and cabbages bought from the local supermarket arranged in neat rows ready to be harvested. You get the idea? With clean water, you can do all this!

They dug a trench to show how the water pipes were connected, erected the tank and put up an outside loo. The bystanders were very puzzled by the pipe that was carefully laid but not connected to anything at either end; the outside loo that had nothing inside it, and that all the water we were using was provided by a water tanker from the Council on standby for the week.

We used Council workers to 'act' as the family, playing with their shiny, clean offspring, making numerous trips to the empty loo, offering a passing motorist water when his car overheated, the 'show off' part, and through all this, they were seen brimming with good health.

We then threw in information about the Council workers from the Water Department out in the field, sweating away under the blazing African sun, one of whom just happened to be our featured shack owner, and how pleased they were to receive their pay checks at the end of the month.

The second programme was scheduled to be shot the following week, and this time we would be featuring the shack next door, who had *not* subscribed to the low cost water offer. The nagging wife would go on at her husband to apply for their water tank, while he spent a lot of time spying through the bushes on the successful family next door. We were ready to roll the following Monday morning, but on the Saturday there was a political assassination in Johannesburg which sent shock waves the length and breadth of the country. Chris Hani, the leader of the South African Communist Party, and chief of staff of Umkhonto we Sizwe (the armed wing of the African National Congress), was gunned down by a far right Polish immigrant called Janusz Walus. He fled but was arrested soon afterwards and a senior South African Conservative Party MP, Clive Derby-Lewis was implicated for lending his gun to Janusz.

There were serious tensions and some riots, and Nelson Mandela called for calm amid fears that the whole country would erupt in violence. When we arrived at the studio the following Monday morning, prepared to go back into the squatter camp and continue shooting, I was quite nervous. How safe was it going to be?

However, as we assembled the gear, no one discussed if it was wise to go into an informal area, even though we had no idea of the mood of the people. I admit to being very scared as we drove in, would we be welcomed or attacked?

In the event it was all very peaceful, and as both scripts contained plenty of humour, we were soon surrounded by a group of curious and cheerful people who were being well entertained.

The happy contented family were still ecstatic with their new water tank, but the nagging wife next door was constantly bullying her husband to pay to have the system as well. She played her part so well, that later she was approached by the SABC in Durban for further work. I had not scripted her exact dialogue, but through our interpreter I explained the kind of things I wanted her to say in her own words. We had no idea what she said, but the massed crowd and Shezi on the crew and the Council workers were all in fits of laughter. It was a tremendous relief that everyone was so relaxed.

I felt really sorry for the original homeowner as she must have been thrilled with all the improvements to her home, but sadly at the end of the two weeks, the pretty flowers were returned to the municipal nursery, the painted stones replaced in the local park, the shell of the outside privy was removed, the pipes ripped back out again and carried off on the truck, and that only left the cabbages which had wilted beyond repair and were not fit to eat. She was of course left with a newly painted house, but only on two sides.

I heard later that our videos were shown overseas at an international water conference and received a lot of acclaim, although we were unaware of this for a long time.

I'd never thought much about how city councils are run or what they are responsible for, but I was soon to learn how the Health, Water, Sanitation, Parks and Recreation, Beach Services, Police Force, Electricity and Road Maintenance, Communications, Treasury and all the other departments functioned. One programme followed another and there were many stories to tell.

The Health Department were keen to use video as a vehicle for educating the local people. They were particularly worried about the state of the cooked food stalls which had sprung up all over the city. The levels of hygiene were suspect to say the least, and the food they sold would have had me throwing up all the way down the road. The smell alone was enough to put you off, never mind tasting it.

Once again I turned this into a drama and concocted a story about a brash young man who comes into town to make his fortune by setting up his stall, a simple idea, but often those work the best. He gets into all kinds of trouble, he puts his food out on the ground and members of the public step on it, but he still offers it for sale. He does not have the capital to buy a stall, nor does he make any effort to construct one from all the timber lying around.

Our hero spends a lot of time dodging the City Health Inspector, since he doesn't have a licence for a stall, and this leads to some comic scenes as he is chased off. Now he does not have any food to sell, so he steals some from another stall, and then the market people are after him as well.

He is now forced to set up a stall on a busy road and it's demolished by passing traffic. That took a bit of organizing. We had to get a wrecked car from the municipal pound and get a Council vehicle to push it from behind to flatten the stall, while being careful to keep the good car out of shot. That drew a large crowd in the streets.

It was all going so well. We were using a professional actor who was the star of a local soap on television and a joy to direct. The messages were subliminal and wrapped up as a sitcom which made everyone laugh. I think it's the best and least intrusive way of educating.

We had a bit of a fright on the second to last day of our filming in the market. The crew were all out of sight of the stall for a few minutes and when we returned, our star was nowhere to be seen. Where had he gone? We searched everywhere until one of the other stall holders informed us he had been arrested by the police for the disgusting state of his food and his stall. In spite of its filthy state, we had already refused to sell to a few hopeful shoppers. It only took one phone call to get him back, but I think he was a little shaken. Did the police really think their favourite soap star was moonlighting on the side?

But on the last day there was real trouble. We had set up a stall in one of the quieter streets on a road near the edge of town, hoping to avoid the crowds that gathered and would just not keep quiet. We were taking a few early establishing shots when we noticed that the road was totally deserted, which was a little strange - not a single person in either direction?

Just then a police car drew up, followed by the mortuary van, and I noticed with horror that the bundle by the kerb further up the incline was in fact a dead body. Our cameraman, Carl, went to talk to the police and came back with the news that there'd been a shooting that morning from the hostel in front of us and they were still looking for the gunman. Apparently he had fired on the hapless victim from one of the windows, but it seemed to me that no one was making any great effort to find him and arrest him. Surely the place should be swarming with police by now?

I know there are several murders every day in Durban alone, but this over casual approach had to be seen to be believed.

The mortuary attendants loaded up the body into the van and drove off, but I couldn't take my eyes off the hostel windows. The hairs on the back of my neck were standing up and shivers kept going up and down my spine. This was worse than being in the squatter camp right after the assassination. The gunman might have been shooting at random, and if he was still there, I prayed I would not be his next victim.

About half an hour later two ladies came out in the street and began sluicing down the kerbside with buckets of water, and to my horror I saw brain matter was flowing past our feet while we were trying to shoot the good, clean food stall manned by our star, who had learned his lesson. It was another uncomfortable day's filming and more than a little propaganda into the bargain.

Africans are a joy to work with. They are so unselfconscious and willing to play their part, even when they are not sure they understand the whole concept of the programme. If we asked them to clap and cheer they did, if we asked them to pretend to cry, you could hear their wails a mile away. They would act out little scenes even though they did not understand the purpose of what they were doing, and I found that in KwaZulu-Natal, the local people were far less sophisticated than those who lived up on the Reef. Not once did I hear anyone asking for payment for appearing in a programme, not even if we had used up quite a lot of their time. I believe that inside every African there is a Will Smith or Denzel Washington just waiting to be discovered!

Sadly I can't say the same for those of European origin. They would go into a total tizz, whip out the comb, makeup bag and mirror and refuse to stop giggling through take after take after take. It was often difficult to remain patient as the minutes ticked by and they fiddled with their hair and clothing. They would also insist on looking to see what they looked like on the footage, and would often ask for more takes if they didn't like what they saw.

It was no good trying to tell them that in most instances they would only be on camera for perhaps ten or fifteen seconds and unless you paused the tape, you were unlikely to get a really good look at them. It's strange, isn't it, how we all rush to see something familiar when it's on the little box in the house, when we could look out of the window, or walk down the street and see the real thing clearer, sharper and brighter, or even talk to someone right next to us in real life as opposed to watching them later on a small screen. Such is the magic of television.

The Electricity Department required a programme to re-enforce the safety measures in their large substation on the southern edge of the city, right next to a very large black township called Umlazi, in fact it's the third largest black township in South Africa. There was always the fear that it might be the target of unrest and since many possible attacks might be made at night, this meant a couple of nights shooting after dark.

The first night went well, as we recorded the night staff locking gates behind them and then checking there had been no illegal entries, but it was the second night I remember most clearly.

Carl was determined to make this programme as realistic as possible, and I had not written this as a dramatized story. It was a simple step-by-step visual manual in safety measures and what to do in the case of attack. I'm not sure where he got them, but on the second night, Carl turned up with a pocketful of thunder flashes and, to my horror, announced he was going to mount an armed attack.

Now I don't like loud noises at the best of times, and I made quite sure I was as far away as possible when they were let off. But it didn't stop there. From out in the night, gunfire erupted all around us. I was terrified and flung myself flat on the ground - remember those programmes in Johannesburg about 'What to do in an Emergency?' Well that's what you do; you throw yourself on the ground.

I lay there and tried to control both my ragged breathing and my bladder at the same time, which is not an easy thing to do. My last hour had finally come and I thought about my children on the boat, my ex far away in Johannesburg and my mother in England and I whispered a quiet goodbye to them all.

So we were under attack? Uh, no. It was the night of some big football finals, and every time the Durban team scored a goal, dozens of the locals would rush out of their houses and fire their guns in the air. At least seeing me shaking on the ground, gave the rest of the crew a good laugh.

You have no idea how many guns are at large in South Africa. I don't know where they all came from but they were reported to be used in every hold up or robbery you read about, and all the others that never made the papers as well. Even when we had been shooting 'Why Pay for Water?' a local man had tugged at my arm and pulled me to one side whispering in my ear to ask if I wanted to purchase an AK47. I couldn't believe what I was hearing and asked him to repeat it.

Sure enough he was offering to sell me a selective-fire, gas operated, assault rifle, capable of killing a man at 300 metres, or 800 metres if you are good at firing guns, which could project bullets through walls and car doors at the rate of 600 rounds a minute. He was not likely to have much success with me, as I'm too scared to even hold a sparkler. However he assured me it was really cheap, but the bullets were quite pricey. Did he really think I would just hand over the money, tuck it down the front of my jeans and hope no one would notice?

It wasn't the only time I made a complete fool of myself over loud noises. We were filming in an Indian township and once again the guns started going off at a rapid rate. Once again I played starfish on the ground while Carl, Shezi and our guide doubled up in fits of laughter. Someone could have mentioned that it was Diwali, the Hindu celebration of lights, when firecrackers are let off with abandon. I stood up, brushed the dust and gravel off my jeans and sheepishly carried on.

I was scared out of my wits yet again while on a shoot for the Durban Tourism Board. They needed a video to take overseas to a large exhibition for tour operators. We had a lovely time filming all the top sights in Durban, with its miles of unspoilt sand, the fun fair, the aquarium with its dolphin show, the rickshaw pullers dressed in their traditional garish Zulu costumes on the promenade, the landmark City Hall and the surrounding rural areas of the Valley of a Thousand Hills.

"Fine," they said, "but we need some Zulu dancing, and to showcase one of the resorts in the Drakensburg Mountains, we'll fly you up there tomorrow." That was fine with me as remember I love flying, but I was not quite so keen when I saw the tiny aircraft on the runway the following morning. It only had one engine, and personally, I prefer two, just in case.

It was with a sigh of relief that they transferred us to a two-engine plane after unsuccessfully trying to stuff the three crew members and all our equipment into the four-seater, that and the fact they could not get even that *one* engine to start.

The second plane was quite a bit larger and we settled in for an enjoyable ride. I was a little apprehensive when I noticed the pilot looked as if he was just out of primary school, but told myself that South Africa had high safety standards and surely he must know what he was doing.

I searched in vain for my seat belt, (I am very well-trained) but it appeared to have left the aircraft. Never mind, I thought, it's not quite the same as wearing one in a car, is it? We took off and flew low over the city, heading west, but before too long we were enveloped in a huge blanket of fog, which got thicker and thicker.

I noticed the pilot seemed a little uneasy, but it wasn't until he asked us to pass his briefcase forward, and then got out a map and a pair of compasses that I began to feel slightly alarmed. I noticed that Carl the cameraman was beginning to sweat and that was unnerving. I knew he could fly a plane, his father had sold planes in Zimbabwe and allowed him to take the controls on many occasions.

I asked him very quietly if everything was OK, and we both agreed it looked as if the pilot was lost, and what was even worse, his radio did not seem to work either. Did he even have a radio? The pilot shook his head, abandoned the briefcase and then asked if anyone had a cell phone on them he could borrow. That isn't safe, is it? I thought in alarm.

"Turn off all electronic devices," is the first thing they scream at you as soon as you get on a plane.

"Uh, is that safe?" I asked as I handed him mine.

"Well I could drop down through the clouds and see what's below, but I'm not sure how close to the mountains we are," replied our pilot.

"No, don't do that!" exclaimed Carl in alarm, while I had visions of us being impaled on a mountain top, and then my imagination began to run riot. I've never been known to be even the slightest bit brave, no one could ever accuse me of that.

"Ah look!" said our pilot cheerfully, "there's a break in the clouds, I'll try to land down there and we can find out where we are."

So we *were* lost!

"No, please don't," begged Carl, "that's a ploughed field down there."

In the meantime, I glanced over to see how Shezi was reacting, but from his relaxed manner and the smile on his face he wasn't the slightest bit concerned. Was this the Africans' blind acceptance in fatalism, or had it not yet occurred to him we were lost over the Drakensberg Mountains, in deep fog, no radio contact with the outside world, with a clueless pilot, and our situation could be just a tad dangerous?

Reluctantly the pilot gained height to take us over the clouds, and used my cell phone to call the tower at Pietermaritzburg Airport. I was so pleased he dialled it from memory as that is not a number I would normally have in my contacts list.

The air traffic controllers, or the people he got through to, must have given him some coordinates, or told him which way to go or something, as he then flew us to Pietermaritzburg

Airport, though I'm not quite sure how he found it.

With a sigh of relief, Carl and I climbed down the steps - in my case I sort of lurched and wobbled to the ground - and we all tottered off to wait in the cafeteria until the fog had cleared.

The pilot seemed blissfully unaware of our terror, or maybe he was very good at pretending, but Carl and I were not feeling too relaxed when we boarded again to fly into the mountains. At least on our second attempt, the pilot could see where he was going.

Of course, by the time we eventually arrived, the dancers were totally fed up. They'd been waiting for us for hours and hours, stretching even the Africans' unending patience beyond measure. The leader gathered them back together from either end of the resort, and they reluctantly shuffled into place with very long faces. Then they couldn't find the drummer. At last they were all ready to perform, but it was the most disgruntled traditional dancing you have ever seen. It would not have transmitted the right message if Carl had shown them in close up, it would have been quite enough to scare off any prospective tourists since they looked more murderous than welcoming. So he concentrated on long shots and close up shots of their feet and hands, avoiding the sulky expressions on their faces.

I don't remember the flight back all that well, but they say you push traumatic occurrences deep down into your memory as a way of coping with them. I do know they rushed us back to the plane as fast as possible as it was beginning to get dark. I didn't even have time to grab a drink or visit the loo, so that meant I was going to be most uncomfortable on the return journey. I wished I had not had so many glasses of juice in the airport cafeteria.

We skidded over the damp grass on the landing strip, threw the equipment into the plane and piled on board. The pilot was already sitting with the engines vibrating and was obviously relieved to see us. We bounced over the rough terrain, turned, and as we headed back along what served as a landing strip, the pilot tried to take off, but somehow he got it wrong. As we approached the end of the open land, he suddenly veered to one side and set off back the way we had just come.

My knuckles were white as I gripped the set in front of me and I could feel the sweat start to pour down my face. I think by now even Shezi felt a fraction worried, despite his in-built fatalism. On the second attempt we were airborne, and looking back we could see the lights twinkling below us from the resort. They were the only lights we could see, everywhere else was pitch-black.

Why the hell don't they string lights along the tops of mountains, I asked myself. All around us I could see the darker outlines of the taller peaks and I couldn't decide whether to close my eyes and pretend I was somewhere, anywhere, else, or if I should keep them wide open, ready to warn the pilot, just as he was about to crash into a cliff face.

An hour later we landed back at Virginia Airport, and it was only as we were taxiing towards the terminal that our (very) young pilot announced, (rather proudly, I thought), that he had not passed all his qualifications yet for night flying, so this had been a good opportunity to gain experience and log up a few hours.

Frankly I would be surprised if he had passed everything he needed to fly during the day time, but we were home safe and sound, and for some strange reason, it did not put me off flying.

16 THE SANGOMA

I was asked if I would like to work one Saturday and help a freelance cameraman capture footage of a special ceremony held in one of the local shack lands where they were opening a new water supply. They would be having a little service and blessing the success of yet another leap forward in making South Africa a better place in which to live. Sorry, I slipped back into 'propaganda speak' there for a moment!

Often small ceremonies and other events were shot to be stored in the archives as a historical record, or we might find a place for it in some future programme. The Communications Department had a whole store room of archived footage, right back to the Second World War and even a few clips from before that. I got to see some of it and was fascinated by the shots they had of the visit made to Durban by King George VI and Queen Elizabeth (later known as the Queen Mother) in June 1947 being driven slowly along Smith Street past the Royal Hotel. With them in the car were the Princess Margaret and the recently engaged Princess Elizabeth, who later that year would marry the Duke of Edinburgh.

I also found out that in 1924, Durban's City Hall welcomed sixty people in to witness the first wireless programmes to be broadcast by the first municipally controlled radio station in the world. To record the time, they opened the window and hung the microphone out to catch the sounds of the chimes from the post office clock across the square.

As early as 1927, the government must have got cold feet about allowing unregulated radio stations to broadcast what they wanted. So they amalgamated the couple of them into a national African Broadcasting Company, and then in 1936, this became the South African Broadcasting Corporation, I may have mentioned them before?

The more I learned about Durban's past, the less surprised I was about her 'state of the art' Communications Department and the broadcast standard of their video unit.

But back to that afternoon in the squatter camp, and the footage the Council wanted of the opening of the water ceremony. As I had nothing planned and the children would be out with their friends, I agreed. We arrived at about two o'clock to be greeted by the chief and the resident 'solid citizen', Busi, who had just been employed by the Water Department to collect the few cents every week from residents receiving the water supply.

We were then joined by the choir, over a dozen well-scrubbed, smartly dressed young girls, some in school uniform, along with others far too old to be in school. They in turn were accompanied by a pastor and his wife, a delightful couple, full of smiles and warm handshakes. They explained they had come over from Holland as missionaries, had set up a small church and this was their choir. They had been practicing for this ceremony for weeks, and they were particularly thrilled that the chief had asked them to come and sing for this blessing.

It all went off very well. The choir was excellent as their sweet, angelic voices soared upwards to the heavens; I looked around and choked back the tears. This was my adopted country, where I felt at peace, and it was yet another beautiful day, the sun was shining, and high up in the sky I could see a lonely raptor swooping up and down on the air currents. Don't ask me what type of bird it was, I can scarcely tell a robin from a vulture, unless I am researching to make a programme about them of course.

We wrapped the shoot (another in-house term) dropped off the equipment at the studio, and I thought nothing more about the occasion once I had written out my invoice, remembering to add in the Saturday overtime.

A few weeks later, I was in edit with Brian and we were searching around for some background music to put in another programme. We didn't want to use the commercial record library as, apart from having to fill in duplicate cue sheets and sending them off to Johannesburg, it also cost for every needle drop or a flat rate charge for so many seconds. There was no budget for music this time, but then I remembered the angelic choir in the squatter camp, we could use that.

It worked perfectly, until Themba one of the Communications Department writers, stopped by and asked what we were doing. We explained.

"I wouldn't use that if I were you," he said.

"Why not? The music is beautiful."

"Yes it is," he agreed.

"So what's the problem?"

"The words," Themba remarked briefly before turning to walk back to his office.

"No wait! What about the words?"

Themba came back into the studio and he looked a little uncomfortable. "Do you know what words they are singing?"

No, of course not; none of us spoke Zulu. "Can you tell us?"

Themba took a deep breath. "We will not be content until every white man is killed in the land of our ancestors and his blood washes down into the sea."

Brian and I looked at each other in horror.

"Ah, yes, right. You have a point, Themba. Maybe it's not the best choice of music after all." I went off to look through the record library.

I thought back to that Dutch pastor and his wife. They obviously didn't speak Zulu either, and I wondered if they would ever find out. It would also wipe the beatific smiles off their faces if they ever did, and it would certainly dent their belief in the milk of human kindness. I couldn't help feeling rather sorry for them.

It's rare that you get away with trying to cut corners - someone, somewhere will always notice - and we fell into this trap in a big way.

We were on another shoot for Durban Tourism. This time they were quite specific about what they wanted. Not just the usual sea, sun and sand, they explained, this is more for those looking for adventure.

"We need to show the different kinds of things the visitors can do, active things."

"Fine," we said, "what do you suggest?" Ah, that set them thinking, but eventually they came up with an answer. One of those wildly, adventurous, active things they wanted was fishing in the rock pools off the shoreline.

Now personally I wouldn't go on holiday to catch fish in rock pools, especially things with claws and teeth, but I guess they knew what they were talking about and knew what normal people really liked to do on holiday. Who was I to question them?

This was a larger than normal budget shoot, it must have been for a really big, important expo. We could have real, live models from the modelling agency and, much to my horror, the clients said they wanted real, live fish as well!

I'd planned to stock up on fish props from the local toy shop, or if they didn't stock plastic crayfish, (I had my doubts about that), at worst I would change that to the 'ocean fresh' counter at my local supermarket. But now that wasn't going to work either if they wanted them alive. Carl knew of a couple in his favourite fish restaurant, but when he went to enquire about them, unfortunately they had been eaten the night before.

That was plan A and B up the creek, so we moved on to plan C. I would pop down as the fishing boats came in the following morning and purchase a couple of live crayfish from them. No, correction - I would get someone *else* to go down and buy the creatures, my bravery has its limits.

Plan C wasn't going to work either. Crayfish were not in season and were nowhere to be found in the Indian Ocean off the coast of Natal. Could we think of a plan D?

Carl was a very keen fisherman and he came up with the bright idea of bringing some crayfish up from Cape Town. He picked up the phone.

On day one of the shoot, we met up with the models at a very smart, colonial hotel just north of Durban. They looked young and absolutely gorgeous, so understandably, I hated them on sight.

Next came Carl, straight from the airport, complete with a large box filled with ice and three crayfish in the back of his SUV. I found it hard to believe they had survived the trip still alive, but I was not about to question their health.

We lugged the camera gear, plus the box of crayfish, through the hotel, past the swimming pool and down to the rocks below. We were joined by the male model, I think he was called Sam, he was the one who would be doing the fishing.

Carl kept the fish in the box until he was ready to shoot the scene, and then slid them into the large, enclosed rock pool. He was not going to show they were in a confined space, but use creative camera angles to suggest they had access to open water and so on. I'm sure you get the picture. We did too.

The crayfish took to the water with glee, and then must have been thoroughly cheesed off when they were immediately recaptured by the male model, muscles rippling in the wind, as he suddenly leapt out of the water holding up one in each hand. You'd think the silly creatures would have learned their lesson the first time round. I could add here that I observed from a very safe distance, just in case they escaped and came my way.

On larger shoots with lots of people, there always seemed to be more problems, and I had an issue with one of the female models, who scrapped her leg badly on the rocks. It *was* a nasty cut, but you'd think she'd been sawn in half for all the fuss she made. Limping like a wounded soldier from the trenches, I helped her back up to the hotel for first aid treatment, and left her wailing her head off in reception while I went off to find the receptionist, who didn't seem to think it necessary to actually sit behind the desk. I returned to see that our very precious and expensive model was bleeding all over a horrendously expensive Persian carpet. She was not too pleased with me as I shoved her sideways onto the tiled, marble floor.

Eventually we got the whole programme in the can (I'm using a little more in-house language speak here) and after the edit, the clients viewed it and were very happy. The clients were very happy for two whole days, until they received a call from a rather irate gentleman, obviously an important crayfish expert, who demanded to know why we were trying to pass off Cape Town crayfish as swimming off the coast of Durban. Didn't we know that further south the crayfish were bright pink and the pale coloured ones lived near our shores? Or was it the other way round?

Frankly no, we didn't. Nor apparently did our clients from the Tourism Board. I can't remember what happened next, but we were in disgrace after that episode. It was no good us whinging about the huge number of awards we had won, or how many other happy clients we could mention. We had got it wrong this time.

I really enjoyed working with Carl, but he could be a dope sometimes. He was another of the dyslexic, creative people who needed a lot of direction, and he had an eye for the women. If there was a cute female under the age of twenty five anywhere in sight, you could be sure he would manage to get her in shot.

A good example was the programme we were commissioned to make for 'Keep Durban Beautiful', as part of their intensive anti-litter campaign.

Our theme ran along the lines of 'If you keep dropping litter, you will make the city so dirty and horrible no tourists will come here on holiday, and so no one will have any work and we will all move away or starve'. OK that's a little over the top, but we were going for big impact here, you understand. We would overlay the shots with sepia and grey filters and make Durban look quite desolate.

We went first to the beach, and as I was sorting out the props I noticed that Carl was shooting a couple of really pretty girls sunbathing in skimpy bikinis.

"What the hell are you doing?" I asked him in exasperation.

"They are so cute," he beamed.

"But they don't fit into this shoot, it's about *not* dropping rubbish." I pointed to the bag of props I was trailing behind me. Inside there was a pile of tumbleweed, an old shoe, dirty papers, filthy rags and a few rusty tin cans. I tried again.

"The message we have to show is that if people drop rubbish, then the city will become so dirty, no one will want to have their holidays here. So, no babes on the beach, understand? Roll the tape back and we can record over it." Carl went into a complete sulk, but he was never down for long. I'm sure he still didn't understand half the time what message we were trying to show, but he loved his camerawork and he was good at it. I just had to make sure we got the shots we really needed.

The call had gone out across the whole of South Africa that it was essential that every family should have a house, clean water, adequate sanitation and a power supply. This was a tall order as the population growth was high, and no one could be quite sure just how many South Africans there were. At census time, many refused to be counted, and in KwaZulu-Natal, they took to the air to record the number of dwellings and then multiplied each one by the thumb-suck number of five per household.

The Water Department in Durban was dynamic in their work and went the extra mile to bring clean water to the many informal settlements which had sprung up around the city. They were well aware it was vital to get the 'buy in' factor from the residents, so they would appreciate and care for the installations that pumped healthy water right to their doorsteps. This 'buy in' factor would work best through education, and if you read the sequel to this book, you will learn how they were eventually recognized for their outstanding efforts.

The first prototype for providing drinking water was to install pipes throughout the townships leading to a large, grey, plastic tank, one for each house, which was filled up from the mains every night, and it was these we had featured in 'Why Pay for Water?'

After a short time, these tanks were found to facilitate bacterial growth, so they changed the grey tanks for green ones. Now don't ask me why bacteria liked the grey tanks and not the green ones, I would have thought they were colour blind, and maybe the scientists did too, and the research probably cost thousands and thousands of Rand.

However, the green tanks in turn had to be modified when it was discovered that some of them were being poisoned in revenge during neighbourhood feuds, so now these had to be made so the tops could not be removed.

As innovative as the Council people were, there always seemed to be a way round getting water for free, either by diverting it, or manipulating the pumps. Citizens chosen to monitor the supply for a small wage, like Busi whom I'd met at the water blessing ceremony, and whose job it was to collect the few cents from water consumers, became the target for theft and abuse. Despite all this, the Department staff never gave up.

To educate the public, they converted a trailer and set up a screen on which they played the videos we made for them. Their visits to the various communities included free drinks and biscuits, and they also handed out caps, leaflets, posters and comic books, all carrying the same messages.

They also employed actors who gave performances in the streets and villages, and I enjoyed writing some of their scripts, always funny, always a story and always with a message.

We shot these plays to be used on occasions when the actors were not available or the budget did not run to a performance. We usually had four cameras to catch all the angles, three with operators and one unmanned static camera.

We were back in the studio editing one of the plays when the editor noticed with horror that on all the footage from the static camera, you could see a camera box with a microphone lying on top of it. Someone must have placed it there after the camera was set up and no one had noticed.

Brian edited out as much footage from that camera as he

could, but we were still left with several shots showing a microphone lying on a camera box, and that didn't look very professional at all.

The only answer was to freeze each frame and block out the offending equipment by using a Photoshop technique and airbrushing a bit of brown for the wall and green for the grass. There are twenty five frames a second in a video recording, so you can imagine that it took several days to repair the damage. It was torturous and painstaking work, and all because no one had noticed the gear was in shot.

The name for a thief or a bad man in Zulu is *skabenga*, and they were hard at work one step ahead of us in one rural township where we were filming the introduction of the first ever electrical power supply to the houses. Each dwelling was fitted with a meter box and two power points. The consumer could then buy a paper token at the local store, push the ticket into the box and receive power until the money ran out. Prices were kept at rock bottom, and there was minimal financial input by the householder, but again, with the 'buy in' factor.

I was going to showcase this from the point of view of the contractors, the Council and a representative of the local people, together with a few *vox pops*. I was thrilled to see that a young female *sangoma*, or witch doctor, was to speak for the community. She came for her interview in all her regalia, the skins, the chicken bladders in her hair, and the metal coke bottle tops strung around her ankles and wrists. It was a shame about the 'Guns and Roses' t-shirt though, but you can't have everything. She spoke beautifully, and gave me an excellent interview.

She lost a little more glamour later that afternoon when I saw her serving in the village shop, but we had a long chat, as she explained how she'd received the calling one night.

She simply got up, left her parents' home and kept walking until the spirits told her to stop. She was then welcomed into the home of an elderly lady, a revered sangoma, who was expecting her and taught her everything she knew. She offered to throw the bones for me, and tell my future and I made time the following afternoon.

I took my eldest daughter with me, and we were welcomed into a small traditional hut. We were told to sit on the floor and watched silently as the sangoma set light to some powder in a metal bowl, and then roughly shook a small leather pouch before scattering the contents onto the straw mat in front of her. There was a mixture of what looked like chicken bones, a bottle top, a plastic dice, a couple of stones and a few bits and pieces I could not identify.

She stared at the formation for a few moments and then said it was a bit difficult to tell us very much as we were not of her culture, but she did warn me against worn tyres on my car. She saw me involved in an accident.

I had the car tyres checked on the way home, and kept my speed down to sixty kilometres per hour for weeks afterwards.

She also predicted that my eldest daughter would need to wear glasses. This we didn't believe, as her eyesight had always been excellent, the family called her 'Hawkeye' when she was younger. Two years later she collected her first pair of spectacles and she still wears contact lenses.

That was not my first experience of an inexplicable journey from home in the night led by the spirits. A few years earlier, I had stopped to admire the basketwork made by an elderly man sitting at the side of the road north of Pretoria. He told me a similar tale. He had been woken from a deep sleep one night, called by his father 'who was late' (deceased), to walk to another town. When he got there, the voice told him to go to sleep and in the morning he would wake to find he had a gift.

The next morning, the man got up, and went to collect the reeds he needed to weave his baskets, they did not grow in the place where he'd lived before, and without any instruction of any kind, he began to make baskets, giraffes, elephants and other animals using the reeds. Now, he was able to feed his wives and young children from the products he sold. That was the most unbelievable part, not that he could earn enough to live, but that he was still capable of fathering young children, to me he looked eighty if he was a day!

If I was pleased with the lady *sangoma's* interview, I struggled with the local residents when I went off to get the *vox pops* or sound bites.

"Can you tell me what you will use your electricity supply for?"

"Nothing, I can't afford to buy stuff like that. I wanted water, not electricity."

"Oh, yes, well right. Thank you very much."

"Ah, excuse me, are you pleased now you have electricity in your house?"

"No, why didn't they ask us what we want? We have to pay for the power! We want free water."

"Right, thank you. Pardon, what will you use your electricity for?"

"I won't! It's another government plot."

And so it went on. It seemed that the villagers were singularly unimpressed and they certainly didn't want to hand over even the token amount they were being asked to pay for any electricity. They wanted free potable water in their village, which was beyond the resources of the electricity department to provide.

In desperation, I cornered a school girl and got her to tell us enthusiastically how she was thrilled with the power supply, she could now do her homework after it got dark, and

214

I had to be content with that.

Since the Africans love a party, a big launch was planned, inviting some of the local people, the media and other Council department managers, to a free drink or two and nibbles in the City Hall while we watched the video. It went off very well, with smiles and handshakes all round. Durban had taken another step forward in bringing upliftment to the less advantaged areas.

We were in a nearby location quite late one evening a few weeks later, shooting the out shot for another programme. That last visual has always got to be good, as it leaves a final impression on the viewer.

We'd recorded a group of small boys against a golden orange sunset, smiling and chattering and looking just too cute for words. Unfortunately, we were not able to use it, as we only discovered in edit that the cutest kid at the back had been playing with his own personal toy at the time, and he wasn't smiling just because we'd asked him to.

I digress. As we were driving past the newly electrified village I remarked to Carl, that they must have come to terms with their new power and accepted it after all. There were lights blazing from every window and doorway.

The truth came to 'light' a few days later when it was blazoned all over the press. The new system was a complete failure. For a 'voluntary contribution', much more than the Council were asking residents to pay, a small gang of skabengas were offering to tap the houses directly into the mains supply, bypassing the meter box allowing them access to unlimited power for nothing. And now the homeowners were using it, kilowatts and kilowatts of it, probably with the cut price electrical products, kettles, toasters, TVs radios, irons, and microwaves that the skabengas were probably selling as a sideline.

It was back to the drawing board for the Electricity

Department.

Since it's impossible to see, touch, taste or smell, many rural Africans have no concept of the dangers of electricity. Every year, there are several deaths, often children, who are electrocuted running over exposed live wires which have been laid across roads and pathways.

One day I watched a group of people get out of a taxi in the townships and not bother to step *over* the live cable which lay on top of the road. We were with some guys from the Water Department at the time, and I asked them if they were going to report it.

"No way," they replied. "We need to stay friends with the community and if they think we have squealed on them it will make our work impossible."

In this instance, some enterprising scoundrel had climbed up a pole that ran alongside the road bordering the township, attached several extra wires directly in from the main supply, and then crisscrossed several cables leading into a large number of houses. I learned later that he would demand regular payments for his services and if he wasn't paid, he would disconnect them. It was nothing more than a protection racket.

I wondered if he had been the guy getting out of the minibus carrying several bags from one of the most expensive, high class tailors in Durban. He certainly looked cheerful enough.

17 INTERVIEWS GOOD AND BAD

While most of the time I was busy either scripting, out on shoot, or occasionally writing the odd radio series for SABC, although these were now few and far between, I wasn't busy every second of the day, and there must have been a time when the staff on the print side of Communications saw me lounging around and found work for me to do.

The head of the Communications Department had come up with a clever idea to produce a full colour monthly magazine given free with the utility bills to every household in the municipality.

Another good excuse for a launch party, and why not? If I was careful I could cut my food bill in half, as long as I attended all these functions and stuffed the children and myself on free nibbles.

The really clever part about this magazine was that it was self-funding. It would go out free to over one and a half million people, and so it was a magnet for every advertiser in Durban, and that paid for all the costs. As it was produced in-house, there were no staff bills to pay and it was a vibrant magazine. It had clip-out coupons, competitions and prizes which were sometimes as large as a car, or flights overseas. There were interviews, reviews, and other articles of interest as to what was going on in Durban. So it's no wonder that it became extremely popular.

I was asked if I would like to contribute (silly question!) and so I was sent off to interview interesting and important people. It would mean me snapping out of scriptwriting mode and into 'article' mode, but I was always ready for a new challenge. The Communications Department had been a lifeline for me when I desperately needed it, and I was only too happy to cooperate in return.

Besides that, I loved working there, each day was different, and even on the days we were not out shooting, the office and studios were always buzzing with new projects and ideas. By now I had my own desk with my own phone line, a computer, filing cabinet and my own coffee mug in the kitchen.

Since I was charging on a daily basis, in retrospect it would have been cheaper for the Council to take me on full time, along with the housing benefits, medical aid and car allowance. However, I did not push for that as I had calculated I might take a serious drop in pay and while things were going so well, why rock the boat? I was able to pay my bills, pay for all the school fees, repair the ageing car and provide all the basics for both my daughters.

Going out to interview people seemed a fun idea, especially if you remember just how nosey I am. I've been told in social situations that I tend to ask far too many questions, and I can only suppose it's a hangover from all that 'on the ground' research.

I didn't think this would be too difficult, just chatting to people and writing down what they told me, it sounded like a piece of cake. But, I forgot the golden rule. I relied on people to talk to me and tell me *their* story, most people are delighted to sit and talk about themselves. So I'm ashamed to admit, I did little or no research.

Now with most people this didn't really matter as they were indeed only too happy to chat about their lives, but what if you go to interview someone quiet and shy like Shaun Pollock? I knew he was a cricketer, even I knew that much, and they happened to mention it as well before I left the office, but that was as far as it went and only a few minutes into the interview I was in trouble and Shaun was not going to help me out.

"Shaun, were you good at sports at school?"

"Yes."

"Uh, all sports or only cricket?"

"All of them."

"So you won lots of medals and certificates even at an early age?"

"Yes."

"Uh, right, and yet you chose to make your career in cricket?"

"Yes."

"Um. So tell me why did you choose cricket over the other sports?"

"Because of my dad."

"Yes ...?"

"And my uncle."

"They liked cricket did they?"

By now Shaun knew he was talking to an idiot. How was I supposed to know that his uncle was the legendary Robert Graeme Pollock, regarded as South Africa's greatest cricketer, breaking records all over the place with a batting average second only to Sir Donald Bradman? His father, Peter Pollock, was also a fixture in the Proteas, the national team, and had been voted cricketer of the year in 1966.

I didn't know any of this of course, and I'd not bothered to find out either. Maybe that is a little harsh as I was only given an hour's notice and there was no Googling in those days, and I don't watch sports.

I battled on but I was getting nowhere. He probably wasn't being deliberately obstructive, but he must have been used to people asking how this or that game went and talking about the nuts and bolts of the googlies, run rate and spin bowlers, and maiden overs and such stuff.

Back at the office I admitted defeat to one of the staff writers and she suggested I talk to other family members, maybe they could come up with some anecdotes from when he was young, funny little stories to flesh it all out.

That was a great idea, so I arranged to meet his sister over a coffee in one of the local shopping malls.

"What I'm looking for," I explained, "is some interest story about Shaun, maybe a funny thing that happened while you were small?"

She sat there for several minutes and then shook her head. "I can't think of anything," she said at last.

"Well, did he ever go and steal apples?"

She looked horrified. "No!"

"Pull your hair?"

"No, never."

"Play a prank on someone?"

"Um, no."

"Did he ever bunk off school?"

"Not that I know of." She thought some more and shook her head again. "I can't think of a single thing," she said. "He was never naughty, and he never got into trouble."

"Did he always do his homework?" I almost shrieked in desperation.

"Yes, always, right after supper."

I thanked her for her time, and walking back to the office I wondered how I could get any kind of interesting article out of this. While I have no time for 'muck raking' journalism, the odd cute story does liven things up a little. That article was a lot harder to write than any script.

My next interview was a lot easier. It was with Archbishop emeritus Dennis Hurley in Durban Cathedral. He was an amazing man, so gentle and kind, he was easy to talk to and I got lots of stuff to write about. His father had been the lighthouse keeper on Robben Island, and he'd travelled all over the world and was quite an activist in his day.

Later, after his death, I received a letter from his sister telling me how pleased he was with the article and how he had treasured it. In turn, I've treasured that letter from her.

There was another interview I didn't enjoy, and it was with one of the leading Indian businessmen in Durban, who had been at the forefront of the breakdown of the apartheid system. He had some fascinating stories to tell.

He had particularly asked for me to interview him as he'd told the Communications Department I was one of the few journalists who really listened and collected accurate facts. That was really great to hear.

I'd met him before at several city functions, but this time he insisted that I join him for lunch in one of his restaurants. I don't like Indian cuisine, or should I say, Indian cuisine doesn't like me. I can't take hot, spicy food it physically hurts my mouth and throat, but however hard I tried to refuse his kind invitation to eat with him, the more insistent he became.

"You can have a mild biryani," he said. "It's just like English food and it's not hot at all."

"Look, I'll try it, but I'm not making any promises. So many people have told me how good your restaurants are, it's just me that's the problem."

He snapped his fingers and a waiter appeared with a large dish and a couple of plates. Eggie Naidoo then covered my plate with spoon after spoon of rice followed by the biryani sauce.

I looked at the heaped plate in dismay. Indians are renowned for their hospitality, and I really didn't know how I was going to get through this even if it didn't attack me. I tentatively took the first mouthful, mostly rice and very little sauce and the food exploded in my mouth like Vesuvius erupting in full flow. My throat felt as if it was on fire, and sweat ran down my face like Niagara Falls, I was ready to call the fire brigade. (Did you notice my geographical descriptions? I've added a little more literary licence here). I grabbed the nearest glass of water and swallowed the lot to quench the burning.

Eggie Naidoo looked most alarmed, I'm not sure he had ever seen anyone suffer like this in his restaurant before, and wisely, he whipped the plate away and ordered me a plate of chips and some dry bread. We were, after all in his busiest restaurant at lunch time, and I was not a very good advertisement for his establishment. As soon as I recovered, he gave me an excellent interview.

Another interesting couple I got to meet were Bongani Themba and Linda Bukhosini. They were our local opera stars, now actively running the Durban Playhouse. Their story was fascinating because they were both from a poor background in nearby townships when they'd met. They'd both sung in their respective local church choirs and met at a bus stop! Quite by chance they were heard by someone who then sponsored them to go to the Julliard School in New York.

When the offer was made they were not at all impressed as they'd never heard of Julliard, and had not the slightest inkling of the prestige and opportunities it would give them. Eventually they were persuaded to leave home and go to America, and as they both had a natural talent they excelled.

It was an enormous benefit to Durban that they chose to return to their home town and introduce opera to the masses, destroying the myth that such music is only for the white upper classes. There are many black opera stars in South Africa today and they are really good.

On location many years later I was playing an Andrea Bocelli CD in the car and Subisiso, my favourite cameraman, was so entranced that he insisted we play it over and over and over again, for the whole four hundred and fifty kilometre journey.

I thoroughly enjoyed the interview I had with the lady who ran the Durban Aquarium. First it was a free entry, and I was invited to go round at training time arriving just as they were trying to teach one of the younger dolphins to jump out of the water and through the hoop they held above his head. He did it beautifully the first time and was rewarded with a small fish of some kind. Then he started messing around and swimming here, there and everywhere. The whole staff stood at the side of the side of the pool and turned their backs on him.

I watched in amazement, for as soon as he noticed, he barrelled over to the ledge and began butting their feet with his long nose, but they continued to chat among themselves and ignore him. After a couple of minutes, they relented and held out the hoop again and with a swish of his tail, he jumped straight through it.

"We discovered it's the best way to show our displeasure," said my interviewee with a smile. "You have no idea how they hate being ignored."

"That's something to tell those people who say such places are cruel," I replied.

"They go into quite a decline on the few days in the year when we're closed to the public, and when it's show time they're right up there by the water gates, they cannot wait to come out and perform in front of the crowds. They just adore the applause."

I stayed to watch an older dolphin learn how to swim under one of the trainers, and balance him on his nose before throwing him right up in the air to the other side of the pool.

I was sent to interview many people in and around Durban and was amazed to meet and discover what a wealth of talent and achievements there was from so many who were not in the limelight, yet quietly had done so much, either by writing, composing, inventing or by making life better for others. With people too, it's unwise to 'judge a book by its cover'.

It makes me quite angry when I see how so many stars are worshipped and followed and their every move reported. Do we need to know what their houses are like, or where they go on holiday? Sure, most of them have talent, but what is really so special about them? Talk to any film crew and you will discover many of these idols can be difficult, temperamental and downright rude. I've worked with enough of them to know. Yet the real heroes who've made a difference in the lives of their fellow men are so often completely ignored.

18 THE RAT IN THE RUBBISH DUMP

The phone rang one morning in the production office. Yes, it was that crowd at Durban Tourism again. We guessed another international showcase get-together was obviously coming up. What did they want this time?

We'd already made a really good video for an overseas holiday expo, which was well received, but times were changing.

"It's too white," they complained over the phone, "we must have more black people in it. We want to attract the middle class black population, especially those who live on the Reef and who have lots of disposable income. We need to show Durban as the perfect place for everyone to take a vacation."

So, our brief was to re-shoot many of the visuals and substitute black faces for white ones. I thought this was going to be so very easy, I really had no idea it was going to be so very difficult.

While Durban wanted black holidaymakers, there were, in fact, very few of them around, but it was July, right in the middle of winter so that was hardly surprising.

I checked out the original script and decided that we could replace the white child in the aquarium with a black one, show a black family dining in a restaurant and show a black guy playing golf.

It was an overcast morning when we set off for the Aquarium. We didn't have a budget to hire actors, and the Tourism Office didn't want to lend us any of their staff as they wanted authenticity, so I decided to take it on the fly. I didn't

225

really have a choice.

There wasn't a black face in sight when we arrived at the beachfront, actually there weren't all that many white ones either. I walked up and down the Marine Parade looking for a suitable candidate. I couldn't use those youngsters sitting on the pavement, not only were they street children, but they were spaced out of their minds sniffing glue. Another crowd of youths caught my eye, but they looked like thugs and we wanted to attract tourists, not frighten them off. As I watched I could see them trying out the door handles of each car they passed. Maybe it wasn't a good idea to bother them while they were busy working.

Finally, round the corner came a black lady with her young son of about seven who was happily licking an ice cream. I pounced, and explained as best I could what I wanted her to do. She thought I was quite mad. Was I really offering her a free tour of the aquarium and the dolphin show? What was the catch? I explained again and reluctantly she followed me to the entrance, but was still so hesitant I had to practically push her inside.

Once she saw the camera, she snatched the ice cream away from the child, although I assured her I was quite happy if he kept his cornet, I thought it rather a nice touch, as it showed we also sold ice cream in Durban - two messages in one!

But the mother wasn't having any of it. She flung the cone on to the floor, much to the disgust of the Aquarium staff, and then scrubbed the poor little mite's face until it was almost raw. The boy promptly burst into tears, and in turn his mother started screaming at the child, telling him to behave and laugh and be happy. The more he wailed, the more she screeched, until at last I had to film him from the other side of a free standing glass tank, and hope that his screams sounded like shrieks of joy. It wasn't the best of shots, but at least you could tell he was black.

After several phone calls, I managed to track down a black golfer, possibly the only one in KwaZulu-Natal at that time, and he kindly agreed to meet us during his lunch hour at the poshest golf club situated in the middle of Durban Race Course.

As he was pushed for time, I offered to set it all up. I can promise you, you don't make yourself very popular if you ask to pass through a group of serious golfers and then four of you stand on the tee and shoot take after take of the golfer whacking one ball after the other, after the other, down the fairway.

When the 'White' golfers saw we were shooting a 'Black' golfer, they raised their eyes to heaven, but when they saw him put ball after ball after ball close to the pin, their jaws dropped. We should have been pointing the camera the other way! Yes, times were changing.

It wasn't any easier finding a couple to have a 'candlelit dinner' in the middle of the morning either. To begin with, even if you explain very carefully to two strangers in the street what you want them to do, they remain very suspicious. There is no such thing as a free meal is there? They will expect you to pull a practical joke, like douse them with cold water or let cockroaches loose on the tablecloth or something similar.

When we finally persuaded a couple to have a free lunch at our expense, they did not relax for a moment and frankly, even though Carl did his very best, they looked extremely furtive, as if they were having an affair, or, at the very least, on the run from the law! Actually, it has only just occurred to me, maybe they were *not married,* maybe they should *not* have been together at all?

Our last transformation shot was to show black management in the tourism industry. This time I wasn't taking *any* chances with casual passersby, so we 'hired' a black

227

bank teller to pose as the manager of Durban's five star hotel, and an African American working as an investment consultant, to pretend to be from the Tourism Board, and that's because they refused to lend us their tea lady.

You don't really believe what you see on television, do you?

Another shoot made me feel uncomfortable but for a very different reason. Again it was a Saturday afternoon shoot for the records, in a township where they were opening a new library and community hall.

As usual everyone was kept hanging about for hours until the big wigs deigned to turn up. There were the usual long, long, long speeches and finally the choir and dancers made their appearance. It was one of those times when, just as you think you are at one with Africa, you are jolted into the reality you are a European in origin.

I was aghast at the young dancers, yes they were bare breasted and I had seen that many times before and it didn't bother me, but these were aged about ten to twelve years old and they were only partly developed. Somehow that seemed wrong to me, and I couldn't decide if the children were happy to dance like that. They were just too young, that in-between stage when your body becomes something you are not familiar with.

It was probably just me being over sensitive.

There was a never ending series of events and celebrations. Durban became a Mega City, so there had to be a party for that. There was an annual photographic competition, entered with more competitive spirit than hopefuls wanting to be chosen for the Olympics. There was an award ceremony for that as well.

We had a City Star Awards evening to recognize all those

Council employees who had worked well and gone above and beyond the call of duty. This always included a play, and one year we had a polystyrene spaceship on the stage, and lots of singing and dancing, as well as a great meal.

We were particularly pleased with that play, and all the members of the Communications Department thought it was very funny. The script I wrote revolved around the 'new emergency number' for the Council, which was 58362938509574632855359938572120 or something similar. We giggled every time the actors recited it, but it was way past the audience who sat in stunned silence. Not only did they not 'get it,' but to my horror, I noticed a couple of them trying to write it down! Since the actors changed them every time, one poor man was getting into quite a state.

When I was first working for the Council, prizes at these Awards could include a holiday in a game park, or even flights to London.

There was an even bigger bash when the International Conference Centre was opened, and again when awarding the freedom of the city to Nelson Mandela and of course, those British Royal visits.

We had quite a problem on Princess Anne's visit as we had been warned that she was not a great lover of the press. Although we were rolling the camera before she even appeared in the doorway at the top of the steps to the plane, she was down, across the apron and into a car so fast, if you blinked, you missed her.

Naturally we had no permission, even if the video unit team was always there to record the event for posterity, to take our crew car airside, so we had to race back to the car park, fiddle with the ticket at the barrier and take off in hot pursuit.

By now the Princess and her entourage were long gone, but we knew the way to the school she was visiting, and set out to get there. Four hours later, after a fruitless drive round, and round and round, we finally admitted defeat and that was the end of that. All we had to show for her visit was seven seconds of the Princess galloping past us on her way to the car.

For my research, and also in setting up interviews with councillors and other people working in the City Hall, I got to know the Mayor's secretary, an Afrikaner with a magic sense of humour, so when he asked me if I would be willing to write speeches for the Mayor, I thought he was joking. This time, he wasn't.

I thought it might look good on the resume, so I said I'd give it a try. There were two kinds to write, one is the usual welcoming blurb, quite short and as long as you got the right information, such as the 'Basketball Team from Baltimore', and not the 'Basketball Team from Bangladesh', you couldn't go wrong.

Then there were the keynote addresses, and remembering how many times I had sat listening to the officials go on and on and on, I kept them down to the recommended twenty minutes. Often the Mayor would wander off the script and indulge in hours of political rhetoric, but that was not my problem.

So I got used to running up and down the red carpeted stairs to the Mayor's Parlour, and at first, the speeches were quite easy to write as I tried to make them as inclusive as I could, and not whine on too much about the evils of apartheid etc.

But as the weeks went past, it became more and more difficult to make each one a bit different. There are only so many ways you can say "Welcome, and this is what Durban is all about," and "We welcome you as we plan together to forge unbreakable links for the future, blah, blah, blah."

I remember one night with a very tight deadline looming, I

was scratching around for something, anything, to say, and in desperation I had a couple of glasses of wine. I don't drink often, but that night I wrote what I thought was the best mayoral speech of my life. I had it thrown right back at me the following day and was told to start over. I wish I could remember now what I had written.

In my time working for the Council, I spent a lot of time in toilets. Not because I suffered any digestive problems, but because the Water Department was working tirelessly to provide sanitation for the masses and had tried every which way to find the best solution.

The most popular and efficient kind of toilets was found to be the urine diversion system, and there were plenty of programmes to be made to explain to the people how these toilets worked, and how to use them properly. Again we took all this information and delivered it up in bite sized chunks, including the usual refrain of hand washing of course.

We were taken out to see the prototype which had been erected outside in a lady's garden. She welcomed us in true Zulu fashion and proudly went inside to collect the keys, assuring us that not just anyone was allowed to use her toilet. Apparently, she didn't use it either, as she did not want to get it messed up. I could certainly see what she meant as I peered in through the doorway. It was spotlessly clean and everything was covered in frills. There was a frilly cover over the toilet roll holder, a frilly toilet cover on the seat, a paper frill round the sand bucket, frills adorned the pipe leading to the urinal and of course, there were frills around the toilet itself. I told her how lovely it looked and she beamed with pride.

But that was not all; she had painted the outside too, in black, green, red, orange, white and blue in a replica of the South African flag.

The original intention had been to feature her prototype

urine diversion loo in one of the many ceremonies when all the big wigs would attend, but the Water Department had to hastily construct a second one, as it was not thought right and proper to have the South African colours displayed on an outside toilet. That was bordering on disrespect.

It must have been tough on the Council, who worked so hard to install new facilities only to find out they were not being used, and were only regarded as a status symbol. How do you change mindsets?

In my next script, I thought that we should include the added benefit that using one of these toilets meant that you could commune with nature in peace and comfort and even keep dry when it was raining! I thought it was a point worth mentioning. Well it doesn't rain all that often in KwaZulu-Natal, usually only in the summer, but I had to think of some benefits, and noticing they each had a roof on them, I thought this would be a sure fire winner.

We travelled out to one of the structures, and I announced that we were now going to film one in use in the rain.

"But it's not raining," said Carl looking very puzzled.

"Yes, I know that, but I am going to make it rain," I boasted.

"HA! Even you're not that clever," he replied.

"Just watch me!"

I got one of the Council employees to use the hose I had ordered, connect it to a nearby tap, instructed him to wet the ground all round the loo and then spray it up in the air so that it fell more or less straight down in front of the toilet door. By framing the camera up at an angle to take exactly the right shot, I swear no one would ever guess it was not real rain.

You don't still believe what you see on television, do you?

I caught a very nasty bug while filming more toilets on one informal settlement, and I know just how it happened. I always provided an individual packed lunch and drink for the crew, as buying anything other than sealed foods from the local stores could be a bit suspect. That particular day we were in a crowded alley where they had just managed to squeeze in a couple of toilets. I slipped on some wet mud and I put my hand out to steady myself, and I opened my lunch box a few moments later.

One huge problem with informal settlements is how closely the shacks are together - the footpaths between are narrow and it's impossible to get a vehicle in. This can make them death traps if there's a fire, for there's no access for the fire engines, or even for ambulances.

Another problem comes when the authorities attempt to re-house families. There will not be enough land in the present townships to build dwellings for all the current inhabitants if they're given new homes with adequate space between them.

I'd learned on the Reef that Alexandra Township had been planned along these lines, with solid red brick houses each with a garden and a fully-functioning power, water and sanitation supply. When friends and relatives came in from the countryside, the residents put up as many shacks as would fit in their back yards and became slumlords. It didn't take too long before the services were overloaded, and the end results were power cuts and raw sewage flowing down the streets and into the river, causing major pollution.

It took three courses of ever stronger antibiotics to destroy that bug, and two weeks of me writhing in agony in bed before I recovered. It just goes to show how tough many of the local people are.

Along with the urgent need to provide toilets, there was also an enormous problem with rubbish surrounding the informal settlements.

Durban Solid Waste (DSW) was keen to encourage the squatter camp residents to clear the rubbish that piled up higher and higher around their settlements day after day. The Department was prepared to send a rubbish skip, free of charge, if the local people would collect up the waste and fill the large bin. DSW also planned a travelling road show, featuring a video to show how to do this, while at the same time, explaining the dangers of decomposing matter and the effects it could have on health and safety. They'd already observed with horror how the young children ran happily in, over, around and through the trash piles.

The storyline this time was of a malevolent fly who loved to make people sick, and we shot most of the programme from the fly's point of view, a reincarnation of Basil. He lived of course, in the rubbish pile.

Once again we had the amazing co-operation of the different Council departments, the skip was delivered, and a few days later the ambulance came too, to take our 'patient' to hospital. I wanted to emphasize how costly it was if you lived in unsanitary conditions.

As we arrived each morning, we glanced in the skip, but it remained empty, even though Shezi and some of the Council workers who spoke Zulu, had explained to the people why it had been deposited right by their houses, and how they could use it. Once it was full, the Council workers would come and take all the nasty, foul-smelling rubbish away, and believe me, it smelled foul.

It didn't look as if the fly was working too well, so I decided to introduce a rat into the story. If the locals weren't too bothered about the occasional fly, surely they didn't like rats. Problem was, where do you find rats, and who was going to catch one for us? The cute, white ones you can buy in the pet shops wouldn't do at all. We needed a large, ugly, menacing rat.

Of course, as you can imagine, there *were* plenty of rats around, but we couldn't be sure that one would obligingly run past the camera just when we wanted it to. Not one scuttled up to volunteer for an audition.

"No problem, we'll ask the Health Department to help," DSW told us.

I wasn't too keen on the idea of driving around in the crew van with a vicious rat in the back, but you have to take the good and the bad in all jobs don't you?

So the following morning, we pitched up at the Health Department's laboratories and were shown a pen full of rats, brown rats, black rats and multi-coloured rats.

"Which one do you want?" they asked.

I pointed to the largest grey one. "That colour will show up best on the camera and he seems to have extra large teeth, we'll take that one."

Now we had located a rat, and plenty more understudies if we needed them, there was just the small problem of how we were going to use it. We were not going to make ourselves, or the Council very popular, if we released rats into the squatter camp, it was dirty enough already. Yet we needed to show the vermin in close proximity to their shacks to push the point home with a sledge hammer, that rats like dirt, rats breed fleas, and rats cause sickness.

(The skip was empty again that morning).

I just ignored the fact that the rat from the Health Department was just that, healthy. There wasn't a flea in sight, but then Carl was not too keen to get that up close and personal. I would just have to mention the fleas and hope the viewers would imagine them. The rat should be scary enough on its own.

We couldn't even practise with the camera and audition our rat first, as we had no idea how fast a rat runs and the moment we released it we had one shot to show it rummaging through the domestic waste before it was gone.

I was trying to sort through my options while I waited for

them to box the rat in what I hoped was an extra secure container, but I needn't have worried. The lab assistant returned with a large bottle, which I thought was going to be the rat carrier, but before I could say a word, he quickly popped the rat into the jar and in horror I watched it wriggle and die.

I was devastated. I don't like rats, but I'd pronounced the death sentence on this poor creature, and I don't even like using a fly spray! I felt so guilty, but there was no time for self pity, because now I had the problem of how to get a *dead* rat to run through piles of rubbish.

I came up with the bright idea of tying some fishing line to one of the back legs, and I bullied Shezi into doing this, and then we were going to pull it backwards and then reverse the tape. Frankly, it wasn't terribly successful. It looked like a dead rat being pulled backwards on a piece of fishing line tied round its back leg.

That night Carl went above and beyond the call of duty and climbed down the sewers and shot a whole crowd of them.

(The skip was still empty the following morning).

Part of the programme finale was to show the skip full to the brim with rubbish and then record the Council taking it all away. Lastly, we would pan the camera round to show a clean informal settlement inhabited by happy, healthy, smiling residents. However, by the second to last day of the shoot the skip was still squeaky clean and empty, and I desperately needed a shot of the locals filling it.

"Look at us," we shouted as we gathered heaps of disgusting stuff and threw it into the bin. "Come help us," we offered.

They declined.

In the end, we had to get in a whole gang of Council workers to complete the clean up and bribed a couple of residents with free toilet rolls, to throw in the odd bottle while we filmed them in close up.

I don't think that programme was ever a great success, as all we proved to this particular settlement was the Durban City Council would deliver a skip, along with a whole bunch of people with cameras, who played around with a dead rat, and then sent in a whole gang of labourers to make everything nice and clean, and all with no effort on the part of the residents at all!

I despaired.

On the final day of that shoot I knocked off at lunchtime and rushed home to shower and change. As the Mayor's speech writer, I was privileged to have been invited to his reception for Prince Charles in the Town Hall. As I shook hands with HRH I thought, he wouldn't be doing that, if he knew where I had been that morning.

Over the next year and a half, I crawled down sewers, went up in choppers for aerial shots, visited sewage works and peered down holes in the road. With so many different council departments doing different things, there was always something new, and it never got boring.

I realized how lucky I was not only having such a variety of work, but also seeing the words I put on paper come to life. It was great to wake up in the morning and say "Yes! It's Monday!"

I wasn't below the radar either. I pitched up at all the main functions, either with the camera crew, or as a guest. Many of my evening meals were consumed at one event or another, and for a brief, glittering few months, I was on the 'A' list.

But things seldom stay the same and change was coming. The original plan for our family was to wait until my ex had completed his business dealings in Johannesburg, and then he would join us on the boat and we'd sail off into the wild blue yonder. I would then bombard the world's press with brilliant travelogues.

Instead, my ex flew off to England, (he told me there was a price on his head), and I had promised him that I would follow as soon as our eldest had completed her Matriculation exam. The three of us, myself and my two daughters, didn't really want to leave Durban. We had a good, if simple life there, although living on our boat in the harbour could be a tad inconvenient at times. But a promise is a promise and I felt we needed to be together as a family again.

I had managed to sell the boat, and there was a leaving party for me at the Communications Department. It was hard not to burst into tears, as they were a really great crowd to work with and I had enjoyed every moment of every day.

I had arrived in South Africa as a primary school teacher, with a rather mixed background in other part time careers and I had been given the opportunity to do what I really wanted to do.

Back in the days when I was about to leave school, no one had ever offered me the opportunity to train to work in television, it was simply not a consideration. No one had even suggested it.

The 1990s was the time when there was a trend to change career mid-life, and make the decision to 'do what you really wanted to do'.

As we shuffled along the air bridge onto the plane, I realized sadly that the chances of me working in the media in England were virtually nil. I had no contacts, no formal qualifications apart from teaching, and the best I could hope for was to find a job back in the classroom, and maybe write the odd magazine article for fun. I'd not had any positive responses when I bounced ideas off the British magazines all those years ago when I began writing.

Just as I had been totally out of touch when I first arrived in

South Africa, I would be equally out of touch when I landed in London. I had lived on the African continent for over twenty years, and I knew I would feel like a new immigrant the moment I stepped onto the tarmac at Heathrow Airport.

The one small consolation I had was the envelope in my hand luggage containing a contract from the SABC for fifty two radio programmes.

As I huddled over my computer in the suburbs of London on a cold, grey, wet afternoon, I thought of the brilliant blue skies, the hot African sun, the dry baked earth and the smiling faces of the many people I had grown to love, and I wondered if I would ever see them again.

I battled with the SAD complex which causes depression with the absence of sunshine, and I found it almost impossible to write and I even struggled to complete the radio series.

It was only when my youngest daughter told me how unhappy she was in London, how she missed her school in Durban and all her friends that I made the decision. We would go back. Somehow I would make a plan to return to Africa, continue to write, be part of a production crew again and fulfil the dream that began when I was six years old.

PS. Yes I know you don't have post scripts in books but then, in case you've forgotten, I'm in charge! If you want to know what happened to Caroline you'll have to read the sequel 'More Truth, Lies & Propaganda'.

%%%%%%%%%%%%%%%%%%%%%%%%%

ABOUT THE AUTHOR

Lucinda E Clarke has been a professional writer for the last 30 years, scripting for both radio and television. She's had numerous articles published in several magazines and currently writes a monthly column in a local publication. She once had her own newspaper column, until the newspaper closed down, but says this was not her fault!

She has won over 20 awards for scripting, directing, concept and producing, and had two educational text books published. Sadly these did not make her the fortune she dreamed of, to allow her to live in the manner to which she would like to be accustomed.

Lucinda has also worked on radio - on one occasion with a bayonet at her throat - appeared on television and met and interviewed some of the world's top leaders.

She set up and ran her own video production company, producing a variety of programmes, from advertisements to corporate to drama documentaries on a vast range of subjects.

Altogether she has lived in eight different countries, run the 'worst riding school in the world,' and cleaned toilets to bring the money in.

When she handled her own divorce, Lucinda made legal history in South Africa.

She gives occasional talks and lectures to special interest groups and finds retirement the most exhausting time of her life so far; but says there is still so much to see and do, she is worried she won't have time to fit it all in.

To my Readers

If you have enjoyed this book, or even if you didn't like it, please take a few minutes to write a review. Reviews are very important to authors and I would certainly value your feedback. Thank you.

Connect with Lucinda E Clarke on Facebook
https://www.facebook.com/lucindaeclarke.author
Or by email lucindaeclarke@gmail.com
Blog:- http://lucindaeclarke.wordpress.com
Twitter @LucindaEClarke

If you would like to be notified when the sequel 'More Truth, Lies and Propaganda', is published, please send me an email.

Also by Lucinda E Clarke

Walking over Eggshells her first autobiography which relates Lucinda's relationship with her mother and her travels to various countries.
http://www.amazon.com/dp/B00E8HSNDW

Amie an African Adventure, a novel set in Africa, which takes Amie from the comfort of her home in England to a small African country. Civil war breaks out and soon she is fighting for her life.
http://www.amazon.com/dp/B00LWFIO5K

Both are available on Amazon in Kindle and paperback.

Reviews for Walking over Eggshells

Although at times heart-breaking, this is not a book full of doom and gloom. There is adventure and humour and the author provides a wonderful insight into the expatriate lifestyle in Africa.

"Walking over Eggshells" is such a good read that I want to recommend it before I am through with it. Each time a chapter closes, I can't wait to find out what will happen in the next one.

That Lucinda E Clarke can write and write well is not in question. This memoir left me breathless at times. She writes of her adventures, misadventures and family relationships in an honest but entertaining manner. I wholeheartedly recommend this book, buy it, delve in and lose a few days, well worth it.

WALKING OVER EGGSHELLS

1 DUBLIN EARLY CHILDHOOD

The first time I tried to leave home, I was three years old. Not that I could have told you at the time, but many years later, while looking at some childhood photos I asked my mother what age I was when I wore the red hat and coat. "Three," she replied and I remember quite clearly putting them on for my first intended escape into the outside world.

It was a cold, overcast day in a quiet suburb of Dublin at the beginning of the fifties. We were in the lounge, and my mother was sitting by the fire listening to the radio. I walked quietly to the door, hoping she wouldn't notice, but as I reached up towards the door handle, she reminded me in her cold, hard voice, not to let the cold air in from the hallway. I opened the door just wide enough to squeeze through and pulled it shut behind me.

I dived under my bed and pulled out a small brown, cardboard suitcase. I'd thought about this departure for some time and had already made a mental list of what I would need on the journey to my new life. I packed three Noddy books, my favourite doll, a comb and a clean pair of underpants. I struggled into my coat and hat and I was ready to run away.

Quietly I crept back along the hallway to the front door and gazed up at the door latch, it was way above my head.

"And where do you think you're going?" My mother stood in the lounge doorway, her arms folded across her chest and she looked furious. Having got this far, there was no turning back.

"I'm leaving home," I squeaked.

"Oh, really, and where are you going?"

"I'm, er….." I knew exactly where I was going, I'd thought about it very carefully, but I was not about to tell my mother, then she would know where I was and maybe, just maybe, come and try to bring me back.

"Little girls who want to leave home should be tall enough to reach the door knob. If you go, then don't bother coming back, I never want to see you again. I don't want you, you're nothing but a nuisance. I wanted a good little girl who would do as she was told, not a bad, bad little girl like you." My mother went back into the lounge and slammed the door.

I blinked back the tears, why couldn't my mother love me? I tried so hard to be good. Earlier that morning I had broken a glass full of milk, it slipped out of my hands and crashed to the floor.

"Look what you've done now!" screamed my mother.

"I'm sorry Mummy, it fell," I burst into tears.

"Clear it up right now!"

"Yes, yes, but please don't be cross with me, please. I'm sorry, I'm sorry." I was shaking as I looked at the mess on the floor. The milk was slowly disappearing under the stove.

"You never give me any reason to like you. You're always saying 'sorry.' If you really meant it you wouldn't do the same thing again and again and again. You said 'sorry' when you broke my best cup, I suppose that just fell too? Don't say 'sorry,' 'sorry' doesn't mean anything to you."

As soon as my mother had gone back into the lounge, I dragged a chair from the kitchen, climbed up and opened the front door. I jammed the suitcase in the gap and returned the chair to its

243

place in the kitchen. Then as quickly as I could, I grabbed the case and ran down the front driveway.

I was petrified of my mother, she was so cold and always so very, very angry, I could never, ever please her. The slightest thing I did upset her, and then I knew I would get a hiding and that hurt a lot. Not surprisingly I cried when the slipper was applied to my little legs, but the more I cried the more she hit me, "to give you something to cry about."

I wanted it all to stop and I wanted a kind, loving mummy, so the only solution I could think of, was to leave home get away from her and find a new mummy.

Five houses along the road lived Aunty Gladys and Uncle Douglas, who didn't have any children, so I knew they had a spare room I could have. They were always cheerful, always smiling and very kind. Sometimes Aunty Gladys would even give me a cuddle, so I'd decided I was going to live with them. We would laugh a lot, they would hug me every day and be nice to me and I would be happy.

I had to stand on my suitcase to reach their doorbell, and it took several attempts before I finally heard the echoing chimes from the other side of the door. It never occurred to me that they might be out, there wouldn't be anyone there to welcome me in.

I was just about to climb on my case again and ring a second time when the door opened. Aunty Gladys looked puzzled, she knew I was not allowed out of the garden by myself.

"I've run away from home and I've come to live with you," I blurted out. Uncle Douglas appeared in the doorway.

"What's this all about?" he asked.

"Lucinda has run away from home and wants to come and live with us," repeated Aunty Gladys.

It was getting chilly on the doorstep and I couldn't understand why they didn't sweep me into their arms and carry me inside. I had imagined that Aunty Gladys would take me into the kitchen, offer me some hot chocolate and then we would make plans for all the wonderful things we were going to do together.

But that didn't happen, they just stared at me. What was wrong? This wasn't the way I'd planned it or dreamed about it. Why *weren't they pleased to see me?*

Uncle Douglas broke the silence. "You can't come and live here," he said.

"You must go home," added Aunty Gladys.

"But...." I couldn't think of anything to say. If I was not going to live here, where was I going to live?

Large tears ran down my cheeks as I just stood there. I could never go home, I knew what would happen, the slipper, Mummy screaming and shouting, I would be sent to bed with no supper, and then would come the silence and that was the worst punishment of all.

Of course I was dragged home after they telephoned my mother and told her to come and collect her daughter. It didn't take too long for the pain on my legs to wear off, no matter how hard she used the slipper, but the silence could last for days and days. When I look back, I think the record was just over a month, not one word spoken directly to me. There were plenty of asides, and remarks made to the dog, about how ungrateful the younger generation was, how badly behaved it was, and how disrespectful it was to the older generation.

Made in the USA
Charleston, SC
18 February 2015